LEARN to INTERN
CEO style

12/18/09

Antionette ---

My fearless leader of the
high school C/o 01 by graduating
first in our class, I still
to this day admire you for
such an accomplishment
that you earned! I hope that
we will always stay connected
throughout our lives! Keep
working hard and pursue your
dreams with passion! Good
luck and keep doing your thing!!

Love
antoine moss
CM

LEARN to INTERN
CEO style

71 Leadership Principles that Got Me and Now You
Money, a Free Graduate Degree, and Respect!

ANTOINE D. MOSS

Wasteland Press
Shelbyville, KY USA
www.wastelandpress.net

Learn to Intern CEO Style:
71 Leadership Principles that Got Me and Now You Money,
a Free Graduate Degree, and Respect!
by Antoine D. Moss

First Printing—December 2009
ISBN: 978-1-60047-382-1

The opinions expressed by the author are
not necessarily those of Wasteland Press

Printed in the U.S.A.

"A Tribute to Congresswoman Stephanie Tubbs Jones"

What we do for ourselves dies with us. What we do for others and the world remains and is immortal.

Albert Pine

The beauty of life is that each person has a unique opportunity to let his or her light shine, despite almost any type of circumstance. Oftentimes, we need others to continuously pave the way with their illuminating light to help us see the light that lies dormant within ourselves. Considering the fact that our society is comprised of many citizens who rely on others to pave the way with their light, these trailblazers have a significant and challenging calling on their lives.

In many cases, providing such indispensable leadership engenders little monetary gain. This is how one knows that it's a special calling for their life because their reward is captured through much intrinsic gratification and little material wealth.

Congresswoman, you were the epitome of a maverick and never concealed your light with a lampshade. As a matter of fact, your wattage was so robust that not even death was able to blow out your light. That's the ultimate difference between living a *life* and building a *legacy*.

A life of a person or thing is constrained to certain properties, formulas, and last but not least, timeframes. However, a legacy isn't limited to any of the aforementioned criteria. Consequently, it's a perpetual spirit that can't be calculated and limited to a set of standards in order to project longevity.

Your spirit still lives today. It lives in the people you so intimately helped. It lives up and down every street or road that you paved in Cleveland, Ohio.

From Ohio's 11th Congressional District to the Congressional House Chamber where you changed the world by drafting legislation, your spirit lives. Your spirit lives in your former staff members, including interns, that had the once in a lifetime opportunity to be mentored by you as a preeminent world class leader.

It's impossible to replace an angel who provided so much love, hope, optimism, kindness, support, and joy to people—especially the underserved. Although your physical body has left this earth, your soul and spirit are still in the air. And I thank God for this lasting effect because I'm using this glowing spirit to continue your legacy by letting my light shine in all I do.

Thank you so much for helping me and your other interns grow, and also for positively impacting the entire world like only you could, through the grace of God. Just as a small way of saying thank you, I dedicate this book to you. Everyday I will give my all to improve humanity, as I continue to survive off of your contagious shining light and spirit.

With much respect and admiration,

Antoine

ACKNOWLEGEMENTS

Many authors will tell you that the most difficult part of writing a book is writing the acknowledgements section. And I definitely share this feeling with other authors. Nonetheless, I will do my best to acknowledge those who have played an integral role in my life during my internship experiences. If you're reading this and feel that I've missed recognizing you, you know from our interactions that I truly appreciate you and the support that you've given me over the years.

First, I have to thank God for blessing me with life and a heart that's full of love and compassion. Without Him there would be no me!

My parents, Jeanette and Larry, have both done their part in positively influencing me to be a productive citizen. Mommy—you worked hard to make certain that Mark, Tyrone and I, all grew up to be responsible men. Can you believe how much we have grown as a direct result of your love, kindness, and protection? Dad—thanks for being there for me anytime I need you, and living a loving life that's worth emulating. Daryl (Cap), thanks for being a great father figure!

My grandparents—Charles and Peggy Moss—I only wish that everyone could have you as grandparents. Your love for Christ is impossible to go unnoticed. The two of you are the backbones of the Moss family—I hope that all of us are making you proud.

My other grandparents Sims and Lillie Simmons, I love you guys. And thank you for your tender love and support over the years. To my Godmother, Charmaine Jones, who helped raise me since birth— all I can say is that you are the epitome of a "God" mother—love you. I will always be your Anthony (smile).

I have the best family (and biggest) in the world! There are just way too many to name … thanks to all my immediate, extended, and God family—brothers, sisters, nieces, nephews, aunties, uncles, cousins—I love you all and pray that we all will work hard to realize our dreams, so our family can continue to build on our legacy that we will leave our future generations to come.

Pastor Joyce McIntyre and the rest of my church family at Northeast Church of God, many of you have been in my corner since I was a child—thank you so much for your prayers and dedication to the youth. My spiritual foundation is firm as a result. And as

Paul said, "I am what I am by the grace of God and His grace will not be in vain." I pray that God will continue to keep you, Pastor McIntyre, and our blessed congregation.

I have had several teachers who've played a significant role in supporting me through my academic journey. Commander Copeland—your effective guidance and leadership skills continue to help you develop and mentor students like myself. Thanks for your dedication to us! There are many other teachers and administrators within the East Cleveland Public School System that played a positive part in my success—thank you all.

While I would like to thank the entire faculty and staff at the Cleveland State University's Maxine Goodman Levin College of Urban Affairs, there are a few individuals I would like to particularly recognize. Sy Murray—a father, mentor, and friend, thanks for taking me under your wings and molding me into a community servant. Dr. Ronnie Dunn—all I can say is that if it weren't for you I wouldn't be pursuing my doctorate degree. Thank you for both your leadership and mentorship. Dr. Mittie Chandler-Jones—thanks for your guidance and support. Fran Hunter and Rachel Singer—I appreciate your hard work in making certain I was able to acquire a graduate assistantship. Linda Pfaff—thanks for taking the time to offer sound career advice, and for your input on this book. Thanks, too, to Kathi Howard-Primes for allowing me to survey your class!

In addition to Cleveland State, I appreciate the guidance I've received from the professors, instructors, and administrators at all of my previous colleges—Washington & Jefferson College, Baldwin-Wallace College (B-W), and American University. Karen Brockington and Theresa Harris, both of you made sure that PT and I had a good time in Washington, D.C.—our experience would not have been the same without you! J.T. Harriston—I appreciate the advocacy and dedication you offered students at B-W. You were truly a blessing and inspiration to me.

The catalyst for all of my success was athletics—it instilled in me the spirit of healthy competition and a no quit attitude. Starting in the 6th grade—Coach Curtis Jackson—you worked hard with the basketball team and made tremendous sacrifices to lead me to winning my very first basketball championship. Thanks for your perseverance. Coach Cunningham—thank you for your guidance and uplifting spirit on and off the field. Coach Michael Ward, Coach Fred Howery, Coach Wyn Hines, Coach Michael Bates, Coach Robert Reid, Sr.,

Coach Bruce Coffee (Jr. and Sr.), Coach Floyd, Coach John Snell, Coach John Banaszak (you really have a passion for developing leaders!)—you all played an important part in my self-motivation and discipline.

Coach Devlin Culliver—my most influential and inspirational coach. Thanks for teaching me how to *Win the Toss* by "bleeding but not dying." You have encouraged me to give everything in life my all. You are the best coach ever! I love you man—keep "shooting your regular."

Thank you so much to all of my past internship supervisors and fellow coworkers. All of my supervisors are listed throughout this book. Thanks for giving me the chance to work under your leadership and guidance. Also, I appreciate each of the employees who helped encourage and develop me, as well! Special thanks to NASA Glenn Research Center's senior leadership that have supported me—Dr. Whitlow, Dr. Earls, Bill, Ray, Robyn, Rickey, Frank, Ken. Sue Kraus—thank you for sharing your knowledge and expertise with me—you are a very diligent worker and beautiful person. I appreciate my many NASA moms, influential male role models, and all of the employees from the OIG, LTID, and HCDB. To Carrie Podway, it was a great pleasure working with you at NASA. Your passionate encouragement and hope of seeing me succeed didn't go unnoticed— may God continue to watch over your family as you rest in peace. Thanks Lynda Glover for your assistance during my Co-op experience. Valerie, thanks for forwarding me the information about the NASA summer internship. I'm proud of you and pray that God continues to bless you—you are truly a gift to this world!

Steve Nissen and Linda Butler—my most active and dedicated mentors. My second set of parents. Words can't express the heartfelt joy that I feel for the both of you. The two of you have been extremely supportive and extraordinarily passionate about my success. I love both of you. I pray that God will continue to bless your lovely marriage!

Laquania—you are perhaps the reason why I wrote this book. Through your *My Soul on Paper* literary series, I've become empowered to write my own book. Keep persevering!

To all of my dear friends, Shaw High School classmates, and other supporters—thank you.

My thanks to Doug Williams, Victor McDowell, James Wingo, and Dr. Betty Pinkney for your input and assistance. All of you provided some useful information for this book. I appreciate your thoughts and support Marissa Parnell, continue to be a blessing to others—my Mimi! Thanks Mayor Luke Ravenstahl—keep doing the great things you are doing for your city.

Thanks to my wonderful editor, LinDee Rochelle. She's always been accessible, knowledgeable, and willing to go the extra mile to make this book its absolute best—I love my new title that you helped me with! I also would like to extend my gratitude to my publisher, Wasteland Press, for great customer service and quality work.

Thanks to my big cousin, Jowan Smith, for coordinating my first book signing! Keep setting the example for us by working hard and being tenacious!

Rest in peace—Grandma Hattie Moss, Uncle Arthur Long, and Chanel Moss—I miss you all dearly.

ANTOINE'S INTERNSHIP TESTIMONIALS

"Mr. Moss was a great intern because he had the two qualities I think are most important to a young person first entering the workforce. Mr. Moss was open and eager to learning new skills, and he was also willing to go with the flow and pitch in wherever necessary, never confined to doing just one thing."

Clarence Fluker
Former Internship Supervisor
American Civil Liberties Union of Ohio

"In real estate they say it's all about "location, location, location." In positions dealing with the public, such as internships, it's about "charisma, charisma, charisma." Antoine demonstrated charisma and character during his ACLU internship that resulted in assignments being done effectively and energetically."

Nichole Griffin
Former Internship Supervisor
American Civil Liberties Union of Ohio

"As I interviewed Antoine for the internship at Cleveland Metroparks Ranger Department, I was impressed on how he handled himself in the interview. I found him to be honest and sincere. My first impression was here is a young man who just needs direction.

Antoine was able to succeed in his internship and will succeed in life, because of his spiritual foundation that kept him grounded and his motivation toward having a better life that kept him focused. He was eager to learn and wanted to experience different things. Since he was so flexible he didn't complain about the different shifts or duties he was assigned. He asked for more involvement and was willing to work wherever he was assigned. He was committed and dependable and sought advice while following through on the things he could do."

Retired Lt. Lillie Blair
Cleveland Metroparks Ranger—
Law Enforcement Department

"Antoine came to Capitol Hill with a keen understanding of his strengths and weaknesses, and was able to build himself into a resource for staff members and the Congresswoman. Washington DC operates on money and information, and since interns rarely have the type of money needed in Washington DC, it is essential that they find ways to be an arsenal of information."

Anthony Quinn
Former Congressional Aide to
Congresswoman Stephanie Tubbs Jones, Capitol Hill

"Antoine performed well during his internship with the FBI because he was able to find the "fine" line between bothering agents too much and not bothering them enough, to get involved in case work. Of course, if he would have annoyed us, we would have avoided him. But, even the nicest agent, with the best intentions will forget you exist and not include you if you do not routinely ask him or her "how can I help?" It isn't easy, but Antoine was able to effectively achieve this goal by wisely interacting with us agents and our support staff."

Doug Williams
Special Agent
Federal Bureau of Investigation

"Antoine was an effective intern because he came to the table not only to learn, but also to contribute. He readily was open to learning new skills and participating in a wide variety of activities that made supervising him easier. More importantly, he was willing to contribute his own ideas that the project team took into consideration. This allowed for a give-and-take relationship that makes the internship experience beneficial to not only Antoine, but the project team as well."

Kendra Daniel
Project Coordinator
Center for Health Equity
Maxine Goodman Levin College of Urban Affairs
Cleveland State University

"Antoine's internship with the OIG Office of Investigations was highly successful due to his motivation, work ethic, perseverance, positive attitude, education, social skills, and investigative ability. In addition to his personal strengths, our special agents also helped him excel by giving him the opportunity to participate in the investigation of an alleged stalker. This assignment allowed Antoine to demonstrate his talents, work ethic, and investigative ability."

Karl Strohbehn
Supervisory Special Agent
Office of Inspector General (OIG)—Office of Investigations
NASA Glenn Research Center

"Antoine's strengths are demonstrated by his knowledge of the subject area he is gaining experience in and his desire to continue to learn. In addition, he has outstanding verbal communication skills that allow him to effectively communicate and motivate others. I view him as a valuable team player, willing to discuss topics and issues that impact the ability of the division and center to carry out its mission. I can't overstate how important teamwork is in our environment. He is an excellent example of teamwork in action!"

Mary Lester
Division Chief
Logistics and Technical Information Division
NASA Glenn Research Center

TABLE OF CONTENTS

"**Leaders** should be the **light** to **knowledge** and exposure as **opposed** to the door to **failure** and **closure**."

-Antoine D. Moss

INTRODUCTION

What it Means to *Intern CEO Style*

"Our deepest fear is not that we are inadequate. Our deepest fear is that we are powerful beyond measure. It is our light, not our darkness that most frightens us. We ask ourselves, who am I to be brilliant, gorgeous, talented, and fabulous? Actually, who are you not to be? You are a child of God. Your playing small does not serve the world. There is nothing enlightened about shrinking so that other people won't feel insecure around you. We are all meant to shine, as children do. We were born to make manifest the glory of God that is within us. It's not just in some of us; it's in everyone. And as we let our own light shine, we unconsciously give other people permission to do the same. As we are liberated from our own fear, our presence automatically liberates others."[1]

Marianne Williamson

---

[1] Reprinted with permission of HarperCollins Publishers. *A Return to Love: Reflections on the Principles of A Course in Miracles.* Copyright © 1992 by Marianne Williamson.

"America was discovered accidentally by a great seaman who was looking for something else; when discovered it was not wanted; and most of the exploration for the next fifty years was done in the hope of getting through or around it. America was named after a man who discovered no part of the New World. History is like that, very chancy."[2]

Samuel Eliot Morison

Why You Should Read This Book

You should be commended for having the interest to read or even peruse *Learn to Intern CEO Style*. This small gesture indicates you have a desire to succeed and let your light shine during some of the most crucial, exploratory years of your life. Considering the fact that many Baby Boomers will be retiring soon, along with the periodic job market volatility, this is a very important book that any serious emerging leader should have in their personal library if they want to get ahead in the "real world."

To understand immediately the benefits of internships, reflect on the following research findings provided by the 2008[3] and 2009[4] National Association of Colleges and Employers (NACE) Experimental Education Survey Press Releases:

> ➤ *The use of internship programs to recruit full-time hires is growing. It was reported that organizations offered jobs to almost 70 percent of their interns (2008).*

> ➤ *At 90 percent, most employers who recruit full-time workers from their internship programs indicated that they are satisfied with their interns (2008).*

> ➤ *Many student interns pursuing bachelor degrees will be paid an average of $17.13 per hour—an increase from previous years (2009).*

---

[2] Reprinted with permission of Oxford University Press, Inc. *Oxford History of the American People.* Copyright © 1968 by Samuel Eliot Morison.
[3] NACE News for Media Professionals, Subject: Employment Trend: Intern First, Then Full-time Hire. March 28, 2008. Web link:
www.naceweb.org/press/display.asp?year=2008&prid=279. Accessed October, 15 2009.
[4] NACE News for Media Professionals, Subject: Salaries for College Interns Rise 5 Percent. March 31, 2009. Web link: www.naceweb.org/press/display.asp?year=2009&prid=299. Accessed October 15, 2009.

> ➤ *Students with previous internship experience are more likely to receive higher pay—organizations value past internship work experiences (2009).*

These research findings convey that internships are invaluable due to their tremendous influence in preparing students to succeed in the "real world." Fortunately for ambitious students like you, there are thousands of internships available in many professions for you to explore. Just as Samuel Eliot Morison once indicated, success is often based upon exploration.

Frequently, one learns that they discover success quite by accident, while exploring for a different type of success other than their original objective. I can attest to this *success equals exploration* formula because during my internships I was able to explore many other professions in which I never imagined might catch my interest. This is exactly what internships are all about. Exploration! It's going out there in the "real world" for short periods of time in hopes of discovering your true interests, talents, and skills.

My internship experiences shaped me into being a generalist, since I have been exposed to so many different career paths. As a direct result, I am more confident in pursuing positions and goals in life that once appeared too challenging or intimidating. For example, my internship experiences equipped me with the confidence and courage to write *Learn to Intern CEO Style*.

A tremendous amount of labor and research went into this book in order to provide the necessary and accurate tools that will give you a competitive advantage in the "real world." One principle I live by is learning from others' mistakes. However, I want you to learn not only from my mistakes, some of which you will read about in this book, but my decisions that proved to be successful, as well. In this dog-eat-dog world, many people don't possess the heart to write a book like this because they want to protect their acquired knowledge for their sole benefit. Conversely, God created me to give back to the world when and where I can because death is inescapable, and as an old cliché states, "The richest place in the world is the graveyard."

Many people die while holding information, skills, and incredible tips for their profession that are near and dear to their hearts, without ever sharing them. What good are these valuable tips if you can no longer use them when you are gone? None! That's why I'm pleased you are reading this book because I want my knowledge to benefit you—the living—in the here and now.

In contrast to other students, I'm not afraid you will steal my position if I share some insights with you. Instead, I believe that the most qualified person deserves the job. I love fair competition because in order to be the best, you have to beat the best.

Learn to Intern CEO Style's distinctness is based on the personal experiences I share with you. If you research most books on the topic of internships you will find that someone in the academia arena authored them. Many are college administrators who work in a Career Services Department or high school guidance counselors.

Unlike the school-based experts, I am your peer. I'm not only a college student, but as of this writing, I'm in the process of completing a prestigious internship in the executive branch of our U.S. government. With six concluded internships in total, I've completed what amounts to approximately fifteen rotations over my summer breaks and during my academic semesters. I have maintained an internship every year since my senior year in high school, which began in 2001. Thus, I will soon have accumulated over nine years of internship experience with some of the world's most respected organizations.

There are certainly other students who have fulfilled as many, if not more, internships. However, I believe the writing of most internship guides still comes from college administrators or school counselors because our peers feel the pressure to maintain an advantage. And where's the advantage in sharing their knowledge? In these pages you will learn more about my maverick perspective on this topic.

Fortunately, this book is drastically different from most of the others on this topic because I offer intimate and detailed accounts of how I succeeded over an eight-year period. And just as they say, "Life is what you make of it," I've learned that, "Internships are what you make of them," as well. Some are more formal than others, but *you* have the ability to customize your internship experience.

You have to take initiative and lead your way to success during your experiences. I'm a big proponent for self-empowerment; therefore, I believe all good leaders understand that their success begins with them. They intensely dig for ways to get things done, as opposed to search for excuses that prevent them from achieving their goals. They are proactive, and know how to attain what they want, legally and ethically.

I coined the phrase, "Nothing is harder than preparation." If you work hard in preparing to complete or achieve something no matter how difficult it may appear to be, you will be able to attain your desired goal.

Leaders also continuously conduct self-assessments to examine their strengths and weaknesses. This is known as self-concept. Analyzing and understanding your self-concept is important when endeavoring to sharpen your skills because you discover your areas that need improvement.

Since you are ultimately responsible for your future, it only makes sense to consider yourself as a short phrase I coined—The Creator of Excellent Opportunities (CEO) of your career. In the traditional sense of the acronym CEO (Chief Executive Officer), CEOs determine and establish a vision for their organization and hire professionals to assist in executing this vision. As a Creator of Excellent Opportunities, you must adopt a similar mindset. And believe it or not, you are in the perfect position to involve the necessary agents to succeed in the "real world." You are exposed to many resources that will help you begin your internship career, such as this book, your family, friends, school, library, Internet access, and more.

You want to pursue and work at internships with a CEO attitude. Hence, you must see yourself as a business, and all successful businesses form a vision, goals, and most importantly, a competitive advantage. A competitive advantage is simply something that makes you unique from the thousands of other businesses in your industry, or in your case, students.

I like to think of a competitive advantage as a "brand." Take Lebron James and Allen Iverson, for example. They are both NBA superstars, but Lebron has a reputation of finishing high-flying, powerful slam-dunks, while Iverson is known for his quickness and crafty dribbling skills. To this end, basketball fans have different levels of expectations for these two professional players, due to their unique brands of game abilities.

Since you will market and advertise yourself every time you network, send out a resumé, and undergo an interview, you too, must develop a brand and other fundamental strategies of business in order to gain the competitive edge over your peers. You must be willing to take the time to invest in your business in order to succeed.

As you will learn while reading this book, the *Intern CEO Style* framework has five primary pillars, you must: 1) Develop yourself as a business, 2) Take personal responsibility over your internship career by customizing your experiences, 3) Consistently produce quality work, 4) Sharpen your soft-social skills and become a "people person," and 5) Always maintain your integrity.

Achieving the ability to *Intern CEO Style* will not happen over night because it is a work in progress. You will make some mistakes, but you can minimize their effects and learn from them if they are used as a form of constructive criticism.

Learn to Intern CEO Style will guide you in developing yourself as a rising leader, so you may become the light to your internship organization, by *Interning CEO Style*.

Tips for Reading Learn to Intern CEO Style

One of the best training and development courses I've ever taken was a speed-reading course with Advanced Reading Concepts that was facilitated by Bonnie James. It taught me that no longer do I have to slowly read a book from front to back in its entirety. I now know how to jump into a book and find the information I'm specifically looking for, as opposed to reading everything. So I want to share this exact concept with you.

Dive in and extract whatever information you're looking for. *Learn to Intern CEO Style* is loaded with knowledge and advice. Some of it you may already know and some of it will be new, extremely helpful information that will assist with your professional development and growth goals. If you're not interested in my experiences and how I came to learn the principles that can benefit you, then read only Part Two.

On the flip side, if you are curious as to how I applied my *Intern CEO Style* Leadership Principles to my internship experiences, then you should definitely read Part One. If you think you will gain by reading both sections, then read on! Reading the book in its entirety will help you get a better grasp on issues or topics for a better overall understanding of the internship process, and its many benefits.

Book Methodology

Although I have gained a wealth of practical and valuable internship knowledge from being involved in so many of them, I would be full of myself if I professed to "know it all." To this end, I've conducted an extensive amount of research, so in *Learn to Intern CEO Style* you will find valid and up-to-date internship information.

During this research pursuit I surveyed high school and college classrooms, read books, met with career counselors, talked to teachers and professors, interviewed interns, and last but not least, surfed the Internet for countless hours—these additional efforts added even more substance to this book.

Intern CEO Style Leadership Principles

One of my favorite books is *You Don't Need a Title to be a Leader: How Anyone Anywhere Can Make a Positive Difference*, by Mark Sanborn. After you finish reading *Learn to Intern CEO Style*, I highly encourage you to put Sanborn's title on your list of books to read. The theme of his book is so fitting for interns because they often feel as if they are unimportant to their relative organizations.

However, as an intern, once you realize that you have the ability to make a positive difference in your organization, you will be on your way to *Interning CEO Style*. As the title of a classic book written by Dr. Wayne Dyer suggests, *You Will See it When You Believe it*. So it is important for you to believe in yourself and use my effective *Intern CEO Style* Leadership Principles to help you achieve your goals and realize your dreams.

Also, it's important to note that it's difficult to create principles that will apply for every student in the entire world. We human beings are far too complex for such a wishful goal. Nonetheless, digest this book with an open mind and take what you think will work best for you; then apply it to your experiences accordingly.

An Introduction to the Internship Arena

"Internships are about revelation. They show you how to work and maneuver in a professional environment. But more importantly, they show you your own character whether good, bad, or indifferent. This crucial knowledge of self is what will allow you to develop a special discernment that will give you a competitive edge over other students."

Derric Studamire—NASA Intern

What is an Internship?

A simple definition of an internship is a program that's structured by employers and academic institutions for the student to explore and gain professional experience and exposure, in a particular organizational setting. The term *internship* is very generic in the sense that it comes in many different styles and formats. When you tell someone you have an internship they typically will ask many additional questions, such as: With what organization? Does it pay? Do you receive college credit? What are your responsibilities? How long will it last? Will you be offered a job after you graduate?

One reason these types of questions are common is because just as no two colleges are exactly the same, internships are very different, as well. The word "internship" is a broad term, just like "college." A simple example is when you tell someone you're in college or thinking about going to college. How often do you hear the following questions: Which college are or will you be attending? What is or will be your major? Are or will you be on a scholarship? How long will it take you to finish? What will you do with your degree after you graduate?

Although no one book can describe or explain the many different varieties of internships, *Learn to Intern CEO Style* sheds light on most of the standard internship types. Graduate assistantships, cooperative education (Co-op) programs, externships, practicums, apprenticeships, and fellowships are all forms of internships. Each focuses on training and working with students, so the school, internship organization, and student all can benefit from the working relationship.

The organization benefits from the student's energy, knowledge, and time commitment that he or she brings. Also, an organization can benefit by training students in hopes of one day bringing them back after college, to work as a full-time employee.

The next section will highlight many of the different internship forms and structures. I think it's important to list the *pros* and *cons* of each type of internship. Understanding this information will help you to better analyze and weigh your internship options.

Internships are great and through them I have earned money, a free graduate degree, and respect; however, they all had their advantages and disadvantages. But I must note that from my experiences, the good always tremendously outweighed the bad. Nonetheless, I don't want you to read this book and think that all internships offer the exact same benefits and experiences to students. Even if you were to follow in my footsteps in one of the internships I've completed, your experiences and lessons learned would and *should* differ greatly from mine.

Internship Structures

Shadowing, experiential, versus hands-on

Shadowing internships primarily provide exposure to students without allowing them to become too independently involved. Law enforcement internships are often of this nature, mostly due to liability issues. The minimal level of an intern's direct involvement is understandable, as you wouldn't expect an intern to carry a gun or arrest angry suspects.

Pro: You will get first-hand exposure on careers that are high-risk, which make them exciting. Consequently, you may receive a little ego-boost from family and friends, who will be impressed, even though you aren't involved as much as they might think.

Con: You will sometimes have little independence and ability to be creative while working on assignments. The reason for this is because high-profile work often requires one to have a deep level of expertise in a particular area, in order to make a significant contribution.

Experiential internships are often offered in a classroom setting and are just like attending class at school. However, they are usually fun and afford you the opportunity to complete interactive projects/assignments, visit relevant places/sites, meet new students, and become more knowledgeable in a specific topic. Some experiential internships are like training workshops that end with a team project, which must be completed by the student interns.

Pro: You will learn more about one or multiple topics. Sometimes you will visit exciting places as part of the learning program, and attend presentations and lectures of renowned guest speakers. You will also periodically get a chance to complete a fun project with other students who have similar potential.

Con: You often have to spend a lot of time in a classroom setting, which can be difficult if you don't care to sit for long periods of time.

Hands-on internships offer students more autonomy and allow them to participate in normal work processes on an independent basis. Assignments are typically reviewed and approved by a supervisor before they are fully completed to ensure the anticipated results will be substantive.

Pro: You may enjoy a great amount of independence to use your skills and creativity. You will also have an opportunity to receive credit and personal praise for your work.

Con: You can't just sit back and shadow or learn with your hands in your pockets. You will be held more accountable since you will be expected to complete tasks that fit into a larger project or mission of the organization. This can be a good thing though because it keeps you busy and makes you feel like you are part of the organizational team.

Paid versus unpaid

Paid internships are definitely a plus. Actually from my experiences, paid internships have always been a double-plus because I received great experience, topped with great pay. The wages I've received in the past were always well above the minimum wage jobs my friends were working in order to support their education.

Pro: You earn good money while attaining invaluable experience.

Con: You will miss the pay once it's gone, but it helps you realize that what you have to offer is worth more than a minimum wage job, since you developed new skills. Consequently, you won't be afraid to ask for more money or apply for intimidating jobs because of your enhanced skill set and confidence level.

Other internships are unpaid experiences. Oftentimes, many of the very reputable internships are unpaid—this is especially true for high-profile government internship organizations like Capitol Hill. These types of organizations are often strapped with tight budgets, but provide excellent experience and professional exposure for interns. Even if it's not a high-profile internship organization, you should accept an intern position because most internships are beneficial whether they are paid or unpaid.

Pro: Unpaid internships can still be a great experience for you. It's important for you to be proactive and develop an CEO Style Internship Plan that will assist in helping you develop your skills.

Con: You may have to get another job or additional financial support from your resources to pay for your college or daily living expenses.

Out of town versus local

Many phenomenal internship opportunities will be available outside of your home city or school's town. For example, numerous internships are offered in the Washington, D.C. metropolitan area, and you may live in California. Accepting a non-local internship will allow you to explore different parts of the world that you may want to relocate to after graduation. It also provides a place to visit that may become your second home when you take a vacation or just want to get away for a few days. This opportunity will allow you to meet new, interesting people, and forge both personal and professional relationships.

Pro: Through your internship experience you will be able to travel and live in another area of America, or even outside of the country, while advancing your student career.

Con: Sometimes you will need to pay for travel and living expenses (e.g. airfare and rent). This can be expensive, but it is often worth the investment for a semester or two. However, there may be some instances when your school or internship will offer you assistance in paying for relocation costs.

There are other great internships that are offered locally (near your hometown or school), as well. This is especially true if you reside near a large metropolitan area.

Pro: You will encounter fewer expenses since you don't have to worry about travel and relocation costs.

Con: You often won't have an opportunity to expand your network and resources outside of your local areas through internship experiences.

Instructor supervision versus no instructor supervision

Some schools or academic programs require students to be under the supervision of a faculty member or instructor. Oftentimes when this happens, you must work to create a relationship with an instructor during your internship. The two of you will decide how frequently you will meet to discuss how your experience is progressing and the types of assignments you will be expected to complete.

Usually, these assignments are simply verbal or written accounts of your responsible projects and level of involvement. They may request that you keep a daily journal, complete an essay, and/or make a presentation at the end of your internship. These assignments should be painless and quite simple for you to carry out. You should be able to provide some informative and fascinating information to them, as a result of your first-hand knowledge from working in that particular internship organization. If you take full advantage of your internship experience, you may become the educator in the relationship.

Pro: Should you run into problems with your internship or need advice on something, your instructor is there to help facilitate this. Also, you usually receive academic credit that counts toward graduation.

Con: In addition to your internship responsibilities, school classes, and/or part time job, you will be expected to complete academic assignments and routinely report to an instructor in order to successfully complete the program.

Other schools don't require students to have a supervisory instructor. Instead, they rely on the internship supervisor to make certain students successfully fulfill the requirements of the internship program.

Pro: You typically aren't required to complete any additional academic assignments for your internship.

Con: You may or may not attain academic credit for completing your internship. It also may be difficult to find an instructor to offer you continual guidance and support throughout your internship experience.

While school is in session (part-time internship) versus while school is out of session (full-time internship)[5]

Some internships are offered while your semester or quarter classes are in session. This can be navigated in several ways. Sometimes it's structured for you to take classes on Monday, Tuesday, and Wednesday and then work at your internship on Thursday and Friday. Or, throughout the week, you might opt to take classes half of the day and work your internship during the other half. These are considered to be part-time internships (10-29 hours or so).

Pro: You can attend classes and perhaps immediately use your learned knowledge to complete a task at work, or better understand your organization.

---

[5] It is important to note that some internships are set for less than a semester. However, others run for the length of several semesters.

Con: You will be expected to attend classes and your internship both, to successfully complete the program. Although this is challenging, it can be achieved well if you have good time-management skills.

Other internships are offered in the full-time capacity, which is generally 30+ hours a week. Most of these are offered in the summer when students are typically off from school. However, some full-time internships are offered during the regular academic calendar year, as well. Great stamina and time-management skills are essential to succeed in this type of internship!

Pro: You will be there everyday; therefore, often treated and considered as a regular employee. This allows you to feel valuable and important to the organization.

Con: You may have to delay your anticipated graduation date. Though most full-time internship experiences are usually worth the delay.

Multiple versus solo interns

Some internships only have resources that allow for one intern. This is often due to funding or staffing shortages, which limit an organization's ability to train and supervise multiple interns.

Pro: You receive a lot of attention and are often treated like a full-time staff member. This level of attention will help you recognize that you are making important contributions to the organization.

Con: You may miss the presence of having your peers around to relate to, hang out with, and exchange ideas on class and work assignments.

In other internships there may be up to ten other interns in the same office or organization. This happens more often in large organizations, where there's no lack of resources and work for students.

Pro: The peer interaction allows you to share work ideas and create a peer social network.

Con: You have to determine how to distinguish yourself from your peers in a productive way, so your contributions to the organization will become apparent. This should be done naturally. You should never be deceitful, or try to sabotage someone else's experience for your own personal gain. Also, you shouldn't go around with your chest out, boasting about your accomplishments. Just naturally work hard and be honest, and your work should speak for itself, without you having to say much of anything—eventually other people will begin to brag about your quality work performance.

Structured to pay graduate college tuition versus no tuition compensation

There are some internships out there that offer to pay graduate college tuition. The most popular types of internships that offer this tremendous perk are Graduate, Research, or Teaching assistantships.

Pro: You can earn a free master's or doctorate degree while gaining professional work experience. Many times students are also given a monetary stipend that covers some of their daily expenses.

Con: Oftentimes, you are prohibited from holding other employment positions during your internship. Usually, stipends are small, partly because you will only work between 10-20 hours a week.

Mostly all undergraduate internships do not offer to pay for an intern's education. These types of internships are more common for graduate school students.

Pro: By completing internships in undergraduate school, you have a better chance at procuring an internship or assistantship in graduate school that will pay your tuition costs.

Con: You will have to finance your education through parental support, loans, or scholarships.

Structured to offer job versus no job offer

Popular internships like cooperative education (Co-op) programs and some fellowships often offer a job upon a successful completion of the internship. Sometimes interns must sign an agreement before beginning the internship stating that they will work for the respective organization full-time for a certain number of years, post graduation. On the other hand, some of these internships are more liberal and don't mandate that you accept a job offer at the conclusion of your program.

Pro: Many times these internships offer great pay and benefits (i.e., health insurance, vacation and sick/personal time, and holidays off with pay). Also, you may have the opportunity to be converted as a full-time employee automatically, without having to compete with others.

Con: Budget constraints and staff reductions could decrease your chances of being offered a full-time position.

On the flip side, many internship programs aren't designed to offer interns a job right after the successful completion of an internship.

Pro: You aren't committed to an organization for a number of years after your internship is over. This is helpful if you didn't think that particular job was your cup of tea.

Con: If you had aspirations to join the organization full-time, you aren't promised a full-time position at the completion of the program. You may also have to compete with outside candidates, if a position becomes available.

Internship Arena Recap

Great! I'm happy that's over! I'm anxious to move on to the "real world" experiences of *Learn to Intern CEO Style*. It was however, important to lay that foundation because the internship arena is comprised of many different structures. I wouldn't want you to become confused while reading subsequent chapters.

To briefly recap, whether it's called a graduate assistantship, Co-op, externship, practicum, apprenticeship, fellowship, or simply "internship," they all are forms of internships with slight variations. No two internships are exactly same. They all differ, sometimes in the slightest way, yet they still share a number of fundamental characteristics. Nonetheless, they are fun, educational, and available for you to learn from. If you find yourself in a disinteresting internship, you must find something positive to glean from the experience because it will benefit you in the future.

I have literally participated in all of the aforementioned internship structures. Some of my experiences have been more exciting than others, but similar to many dedicated leaders, I harvested something constructive and unique from every internship. Someone once said, "In life you either win or learn (not lose)." To this end, when creating the light bulb, Thomas Edison said, "Even when I failed I succeeded."

You must develop and maintain this same mentality if you want to lead your way to success while *Interning CEO Style*. The following short article by a recruitment expert, Dr. Herbert C. Smith, "Managing Yourself for Success,"[6] does a good job of reinforcing the importance of the high levels of confidence and resilience that are needed to be successful as a *CEO Style Intern*.

At the core of modern organizations are talented people. They have always been and will continue to be the key asset for institutions.

In our recruiting practice, we maintain that the most important and valuable asset of any organization are human resources. Our objective is helping people to be successful and understand the concept of self-development as an important tool.

Managing yourself for success is the critical next step for personal, academic and career enhancement. It begins with knowing yourself. For the first time in history, we live in a period of exceptional opportunity for managing yourself for success. The rise of online universities and education programs [and internships][7] , the acceptance of entrepreneurship and business start-ups, the growth of small, family-owned businesses, and the conglomerates with exceptional separation agreements and compensation packages, all contribute to the opportunity for individuals to take new intelligent risks, fund new ventures, and establish multiple careers. Today, if you have the knowledge, guts, determination, ambition, and fundamental smarts, you can rise to the top of your preferred choice of work, regardless of where you began.

It's important to understand that available opportunity requires that you take total responsibility for your growth and development. Many individuals still believe it's the duty of the organization to manage the careers of people who are employed. Not so. You have the responsibility for being your own CEO. You should begin today to carve out the place you desire in the organization. You must know when to change course. You must keep learning, growing and being productive for the rest of your life. Imagine; college graduates today have more than 50 years of work life ahead of them. How long will you contribute to your own development?

To become and remain a high performer, you must become comfortable with yourself, know where you fit in the organization and trust your instincts, as you develop a deep and genuine understanding of who you are, what you know, how

---

[6] Diversity MBA Magazine, Top 50 Companies. Spring 2008, Volume 2 Issue 2 Page 50.
[7] "And internships" was added to the article by the author.

you learn, what your strengths are, your values, and where you can make the greatest contribution. Managing yourself for success requires a focus on achieving pure excellence. You will have to continue to reinvent yourself. You will have to make something different out of yourself. It isn't enough to just find a new job or new ways of doing things.

Decide today to take charge of your future. Knowing what you have done will prepare you for understanding what you have learned and how you perform.

Intern CEO Style
Leadership Principles

- ➤ ***Intern CEO (Creator of Excellent Opportunities) Style.*** There are five primary pillars to *Interning CEO Style*, you must: 1) Develop yourself as a business, 2) Take personal responsibility over your internship career by customizing your experiences, 3) Consistently produce quality work, 4) Sharpen your soft-social skills and become a "people person," and 5) Always maintain your integrity. Be mindful that this requires time, as well as personal sacrifices and investments.

- ➤ **Discover your self-concept.** Learn who you are, which values are important to you, and last but not least, your strengths and weaknesses. Work continually to improve them both to develop your character.

- ➤ **Develop your brand.** Immediately formulate and then convey to people what your competitive advantage is. Work hard continuously to sharpen your brand.

PART ONE

Internship Guidance and Advice from My Most Exciting Experiences

In this part of the book, I will provide an overview of my internship experiences while sharing some advice with you throughout, in a suspenseful anecdotal style. At the conclusion of each chapter will be all of the *Intern CEO Style* Leadership Principles that are available for you to immediately put into practice.

Although I will share a lot of knowledge and advice with you, be mindful that applying this information takes some effort on your behalf. Just as Colin Powell once indicated, "There are no secrets to success. It is the result of preparation, hard work, and learning from failure."

Good luck and have fun while *Learning to Intern CEO Style*!

Pride that got Me from Nowhere to Everywhere

"Pride is an admission of weakness; it secretly fears all competition and dreads all rivals."

Fulton J. Sheen

"If at first you don't succeed, try, try, try again!"

Thomas H. Palmer

"Never let anyone believe in you more than you believe in yourself."

Antoine D. Moss

My Prideful Introduction to the Internship Arena

It was the year 2000 when I was introduced to the internship arena, as a high school student. I heard about different internship opportunities and more often than not, never actively pursued them. With each announcement of an internship opening, I responded with only mild interest.

To my credit, most of the teachers and administrators did not promote the significance of an internship experience to a great degree, which contributed to my lack of interest. However, the biggest factor in failing to apply for internships was *pride*—I would rather not try, and continue in mediocrity than believe in my abilities and talents to excel. I convinced myself there would probably be so many students applying for the internship position that it would be impossible for me to get it.

Aside from my personal bias, other people may feel as if there are so many distractions that the average student encounters, which make it difficult for them to understand what's truly important and what's not. This is a natural dilemma for many students who struggle with an identity crisis, and simply become followers of the pack.

Generally speaking, the more popular packs or *social networks* are, the less likely these students will be interested in academics, let alone acquiring an internship.

The groups I associated with were no exception to this popular belief. Not atypically, my high school popularity rested with my outgoing personality, participation in sports, and good academic standing. But no one within my social network participated in internships. However, I eventually understood the essence of being a maverick and bucking the trend.

"Maverick" is the one word I teach to many students when I speak to them during career day events. In my office space at work hangs a very large sheet of construction paper that reads:

Dear Antoine,

We really enjoyed your visit to our classroom. You really taught us a lot about NASA. Thanks for teaching us to be successful and to be a maverick. You were great. Please come again! Please!

Love, Students from Hope Academy Broadway.

I read this letter every so often and it encourages me to continue the good work I do within my community, in hopes of empowering others to become mavericks. Usually when I share this word with adults they reminisce on an old action-western television series named *Maverick. Maverick's* main characters were risky gamblers who had to heroically get themselves and others out of many difficult situations.

However, I define a maverick as someone who does not agree with the popular crowd or traditional way of doing things. Instead, they are individuals who think for themselves and decide that they will create their own opinions, ideas, and actions, for the better of any task or situation—a Creator of Excellent Opportunities. Simply put, a maverick is a positive leader, not a follower.

Becoming a maverick in high school made me visible in a sea of students—or more to the point, I stuck out like a sore thumb! I developed a tendency to seek new information and experiences. I was receptive and hungry for knowledge, and understood that I should try to learn as much as I could.

Consequently, I actively embraced diversity so my opportunities would be plenty and I could learn from others. It was a developmental process for me. I refer to it as a process because there is no point ever in life that anyone reaches and says bingo, "I now know and have it all." Learning is a lifelong journey that must be actively pursued by you—and no one else can do it for you.

This brings me back to my point that there's a shared responsibility as to why some students aren't interested in internships. I place most of the burden on the student because leaders are supposed to keep their eyes and ears open for useful information. As student-leaders seek excellence, they should put their self-conscious pride aside and talk to people who were once in their shoes. During these sorts of knowledge-seeking adventures, it should come up somewhere that internships are advantageous for students. This is where the additional edge over your peers comes from—the internship.

Pride and Dealing with Internship Rejection
While a junior in high school, my criminal justice instructor, Commander James Copeland, was aware of my leadership attributes even before I recognized them. As a result, he encouraged me to apply for an internship with the American Civil Liberties Union (ACLU) of Ohio. Of course, my initial response was similar to the average disinterested student. However, it didn't take long before the maverick in me emerged.

I became curious about exactly what an internship encompassed. So I began to ask Commander Copeland questions on a daily basis, in order to better understand the process and advantages of having internship experience. After he explained all of this to me, similar as I do here for you, I eventually put two and two together and figured out that this internship thing was the way to go.

On multiple occasions, I stayed late after class to complete the application for the ACLU summer internship. Commander Copeland carefully walked me through the comprehensive application until I submitted the document. Soon after, on a daily basis, he asked if I had heard anything from the ACLU. I kept him posted and prayed that any day I would hear the good news about my acceptance into the program.

Finally, one day during a follow-up phone call to the ACLU, they advised me of the status of my application. I learned of my non-acceptance into their summer internship program. I was disappointed, but not too upset because like I stated earlier, deep down inside I thought "people like me" would never actually attain such a position. I believed that only the super-smart students, who had no social life, mastered the process of being accepted into internships. After the rejection I went on with my life, working during the summer, while conditioning for the upcoming football season that began late in the summer.

I didn't realize how much pride in my own abilities I had until the last semester of my senior year. Commander Copeland asked me *again* to apply for the summer internship with the ACLU.[8] I thought he was joking with me because there was absolutely no way in the world this prideful, popular, and athletic senior was going to apply again to an internship that already had rejected him.

My attitude was that I wouldn't beg anyone to offer me a position. I will admit, I was extremely prideful and felt I was too good to go through another application process. I told Commander Copeland that I tried once and it was pointless to try again.

However, the maverick in Antoine materialized. I was reminded of the cliché, "If at first you don't succeed, try, try, try again." And this is exactly what I did. Similar to another life observation by Thomas Edison, "Even when I fail, I succeed; in the pursuit of creating the light bulb I've learned 50,000 ways not to make a light bulb." I eventually reapplied and in the process, had learned one way I should not apply for the internship position.

---

[8] Commander Copeland was still my instructor because at Shaw High School the criminal justice program is a two-year college preparation course.

It was like Commander Copeland was a genius. He told me not to hand write the application this time around. Instead, he strongly suggested that I type it. I did just this—and took extra time out of my jam-packed day to complete the application with more care.

Since guys often don't take office administration classes, this was my first real encounter with using a typewriter, and did it take me for a ride! I made many mistakes, but was determined to successfully finish typing the application, and guess what? The extra effort worked! A couple of weeks after submission I was notified that I had attained the position. This is when I promised myself I would, "Never let anyone believe in me more than I believed in myself."

Commander Copeland didn't *have* to spend so much time convincing me that I was a good fit and possessed the leadership capabilities that would get me the position. However, it was a two-way street. I had to swallow my pride and listen to the person who had been in my shoes. I can distinctly remember one of Commander Copeland's favorite lines, "I got mine and if you listen to me I will help you get yours; but it's up to you to follow my instructions. No matter what happens and whether you get yours or not, I will still always have mine." This means that it's a two-way street and *you* have to decide that you will become successful with your God-given talents and other tools you acquire along the way.

As Hafiz once said, "You have so many gifts left unopened from your birthday." I encourage you to unwrap all of your birthday talents you have and put them to use!

Teachers and administrators can encourage you to apply for internships, but you have to be receptive and proactive during your internship career. I truly appreciated Commander Copeland's patience and willingness to assist me in applying for the ACLU internship. But of course, you should learn from my first mistake and not wait for an instructor to push you to apply for internships. I was blessed by Commander Copeland and his faith in me; but every teacher isn't like him, so take the initiative and go inquire about internships on your own. If you just so happen to need a nudge, count this book as your first push!

Whether you are a popular, stand-out student or not, after reading this book you should be equipped with the necessary knowledge that will help you develop an advantage over your peers through internships. I'm confident in saying this because I've experienced a great deal as an intern—and as a result, I know what it takes to be a maverick and succeed in the internship arena. However, it's important to note that you may not get *every* internship you apply for. The trick is to apply to as many as possible. And once you score one, be ready to effectively contribute to your organization, learn, and last but certainly not least, have some fun!

My Internship with the American Civil Liberties Union (ACLU) of Ohio

The basic structure of this internship was:

Experiential	**Part-time—Summer**
Paid	**Multiple interns**
Local	**No paid tuition**
No instructor supervision	**No job offer**
No academic credit	

The Start of My Very First Internship

It goes without saying that I was nervous to begin my very first internship. Yet, I was excited to be involved with something new that might give me an edge over my peers. The program was run during the course of the summer, which made for even more fun, and better concentration on it since school wasn't in session. To top this, it paid well above minimum wage and I only had to report there four days a week, five hours a day. It was a very busy summer, as I worked out intensely in preparation for my first college football season, and also worked as a bus boy at a hotel restaurant. All of these activities helped me stay focused though, because I didn't have much time to goof off.

This was a classroom setting internship with approximately twelve participating students from several local high schools. It was my first real interaction with students from other schools in an academic environment. Usually, playing school sports was my only activity with unfamiliar students. Just as I competed on the sports level with other schools' best athletes, I carried this same competitive spirit when we were instructed to compete in group intellectual assignments during our internship experience.

As with several of my internships, when applying, I had no clue as to what the ACLU's mission was or what it represented. This was before I learned the skill of researching an organization, prior to being hired. The theme of this internship program was censorship and the Bill of Rights. Again, I was clueless—this time about the definition of censorship. However, by the completion of the program, I had a sound understanding of censorship *and* the ACLU.

If you are unfamiliar with the term censorship, it simply means to modify, edit, or exclude something from a particular context. For example, certain television programs are censored during the day, while other nighttime programs are uncensored. Since children generally watch daytime television, the shows that are unsuitable for them are broadcast at night while they are *supposedly* asleep.

By the end of the program and still to this day, I can cite the Bill of Rights. Can you? If not, I encourage you to do so because you will become more empowered when you have a basic understanding of our national Constitution. Many citizens feel powerless—until they read this prestigious document and learn that we actually have civil rights, which are protected by the Constitution.

Coupled with classroom learning, we had the opportunity to hear from speakers who dealt with civil issues on a daily basis. We also visited prominent government locations, such as the Ohio Supreme Court, to acquire first-hand insights on the operations of civil rights related organizations. We all were essentially mandated to write down three questions and ask at least one, whenever a guest spoke to us.

This was a good task because it helped us overcome some fears we possessed when questioning others. As you may do in your classes, I thought that a lot of the questions I came up with were stupid before I even asked them. I eventually learned that my questions and inquiries were better than I thought when the speaker would support me by stating, "That was a good question, Antoine." I definitely discovered that no question is stupid if it helps me to better understand something.

The only time I felt stupid was when I had a question that I was too afraid to ask, and left without knowing the answer. Now *that* was stupid! I missed out on an opportunity to receive free knowledge.

This brings me to another point for you. Be curious and ask many questions while you are in class or working at your internship. If you ask a question of someone outside of school, you are receiving free knowledge—by the same token, if you are in college, you or your guardians are paying for you to become more knowledgeable. So be inquisitive and ask questions *whenever* you're curious!

During this internship we also learned to become activists within our community. There were several civilly related functions that transpired during this particular summer and we participated in some of them on a voluntary basis.

We were given the opportunity to staff booths at festivals and distribute information about the ACLU. We even marched in a civil liberties parade; and yes of course, it literally rained on our parade. But we still marched forth as planned. And on a voter's registration drive with voter registration applications in hand, we diligently canvassed the community and encouraged citizens to register to vote.

The program included instruction by three talented young college students (Nichole, Clarence, and Briandi), who had a passion to educate younger students. For example, they were intelligent and formulated many fun and interactive learning assignments that engaged us in creative learning. They facilitated a mock trial that served as the concluding assignment, in which all of the interns participated.

Conducted in an actual courtroom, we were split into two teams, the defense and prosecution, to prepare for the mock trial. We all primed intensely and I, once again, thought of it as an athletic competition, especially because at that time I was interested in enrolling in law school. After intense preparation, on the day of the mock trial we "suited up" as lawyers and went to trial. I can't recall who won, but I do remember that it was tons of fun!

This internship experience was right up my alley because I was paid to learn and network with other top students and professionals. I'm grateful for the paychecks I received because I made more than $7 an hour when minimum wage was just $5.15. I was very fortunate to have had this paid internship experience, where I first learned the value of internships. If the internship had been advertised as unpaid, I *definitely* would not have attempted to apply for the program. And in turn, probably would have never pursued future internships; especially the unpaid ones.

I continue to be in contact with all of my student-teachers from this program and we all inspire one another to achieve even more success. Perhaps the most important lesson I learned from this internship was the power of building healthy relationships and networks. I say this because Clarence helped me to attain another competitive internship that I talk about in a later chapter.

In conversation with one of the student instructors a few years later, they expressed that the ACLU had submitted a budget for 11 interns, but reconfigured the program for my participation. They had already selected their students, but after my interview I was considered a very attractive applicant—so they hired me. Persistence pays off!

Don't ever let your pride (or lack of) cause you to tell yourself no—let someone else tell you no. Even if you don't feel as if you're qualified for a particular internship, apply and let the organization tell you that you are unqualified. You may or may not get the position if you apply. But you definitely will not acquire an internship if you fail to apply yourself. If would have succumbed to my lack of self-confidence and misplaced pride (fear of rejection) by not applying, I would have severely limited my future internship and career opportunities—make sure you don't fall into this trap as a *CEO Style Intern*.

Intern CEO Style
Leadership Principles

> **Be proactive, and utilize your resources while pursuing internship opportunities.** Take personal responsibility and ask your resources for help. Don't sit back and wait for someone to get you excited and hyped-up to complete an internship. Notify your resources (family members, friends, librarians, school administrators, etc.) and express your interest to them about acquiring an internship. They may be able to direct you to some excellent internship opportunities. Also, don't forget to use social networking sites like LinkedIn or Facebook for internship announcements or information.

> **Type your applications and forms.** Where possible, type or use other helpful computer software to complete all of the application forms and documents. This gives your application a professional presentation and demonstrates that you are serious about acquiring the position.

> **Let go of your pride.** Never let pride stop you from accomplishing or pursuing your goals. You must be humble and willing to sacrifice some things, in order to advance your career.

> **Be confident and believe in yourself.** "Never let anyone believe in you more than you believe in yourself," during your internship journey. If someone tells you that you can do something, believe them. If they support their belief in you by going out of their way for you in one fashion or another, accept their confidence in you and don't feel as if you aren't smart or skilled enough. Like the Nike logo says, "Just do it"! Be careful not to be arrogant though while displaying your confidence—all you have to do is produce quality work while maintaining your integrity, and other people will eventually brag about your talent and skills.

32

➤ **Thank everyone.** Contact every person who helped you attain an internship position and thank them for their wonderful support.

➤ **Learn from your failures.** Whether it be applying to internships or performing during them, learn from your unsuccessful attempts. If you are rejected or get knocked down, get back up and try again a different way.

Young and Inexperienced: An Introduction to the "Real World"

"Never let inexperience get in the way of ambition."

Terry Josephson

"The barrier between success is not something which exists in the real world: it is composed purely and simply of doubts about ability."

Franklin D. Roosevelt

My Internship with the Cleveland Metroparks Ranger—Law Enforcement Department

The basic structure of this internship was:

Shadowing	Full-time—Two summers
Paid	Multiple interns
Local	No tuition paid
No instructor supervision	No job offer
No academic credit	

An Introduction to the Cleveland Metroparks Ranger—Law Enforcement Department

Once again, Commander Copeland encouraged me to pursue an internship. This time it was with a local county law enforcement agency, the Cleveland Metroparks Ranger Department. I was in my last semester as a college freshman when he called and shared information with me about this opportunity. While we talked, I realized I had no clue as to what in the world a park ranger's responsibilities were. However, as you may have discovered by now, I'm an opportunist, so of course I applied for the position.

I've learned that when successful people offer me advice, it's my duty to consider using it. I have gone into some of my experiences blindly, but as Martin Luther King said, "I take the first step in faith. I may not be able to see the whole staircase, but I at least take the first step." On nearly every occasion that I took a blind step, things turned out to be better than I expected—have faith in yourself and take the step!

Contrary to the internship with the ACLU of Ohio, this experience offered more direct exposure to the "real world." It was a very different type of internship because I was mostly out in the field with the rangers, as opposed to completing classroom assignments.

A Cleveland Metroparks Ranger is a fully commissioned police officer, who's responsible for securing and maintaining safety within a county park system. The department is constructed of units such as, Mounted, Enforcement, Traffic, Bicycle, Dive, and K-9. Each unit serves a distinct purpose in preserving the integrity of the Cleveland Metroparks.

After learning more about this, I couldn't believe how much illegal activity goes on inside of a park. One common crime revolves around drugs. People who sell or use drugs often visit parks because they're perceived to be a safe haven for such illicit activities. These individuals utilize the remote, wooded areas of parks as a meeting place to engage in drug usage, and frequently conduct drug transactions. Of course, drugs are only one type of crime—but there are many others that occur for which the need for police officers is great. Popular opinion is that cops on city streets are more aggressive and widespread than park rangers, so the probability of being pulled over or detained is less.

The Intimidating Application and Interviewing Process in the "Real World"

In May 2002, I contacted the Ranger Department to inquire about a summer internship position. It was requested that I visit the Metroparks' administrative building to complete an application. Upon my arrival, I was greeted by many of my high school classmates. I didn't know they would be there and was a little nervous because I thought that only one of us would be offered a position. We all waited in the lobby area until we were escorted to a different room so we could complete our applications. When finished with the application, we were sent home to anxiously await a phone call requesting our return for an interview.

A week or so passed and I received my call to come in and undergo the interview process. I didn't have many business professional clothes at the time, so I contacted my grandfather and asked for his help. He gladly offered me one of his shirts and a tie, as he would grant any favor to see me succeed.

The date for the interview arrived and though excited, I was ready to get it over with. At the administrative building, I sat in the lobby until I was called to be escorted by an official. After a short period of time there, I was escorted to the boardroom where the interviews were being conducted. My immediate thought was, "WHOA!" This was my first true introduction to the "real world."

Unlike my one-on-one interview for the ACLU internship position, when I walked into the room for this Metroparks internship, there were eight eyeballs gazing curiously at me. Two individuals were from the Human Resources Department and the other two were the Deputy Chief, and a stern lady named Lieutenant Blair. The latter two representatives were wearing police uniforms, with their guns attached to their hips. Intimidated was an understatement!

At this point I was more nervous than an actual criminal who had just robbed a local city bank. However, I knew I couldn't display fear because these cops would sense it in a heartbeat, just as they do everyday with suspicious criminals. I quickly thought about how my grandmother would often tell me to relax and focus on my goals without being intimidated by them. This calmed my nerves a little, and I was ready to undergo the interview.

When the interview process began, I was told to simply be myself and not be nervous. Even though I tried to hide my anxiety, I guess they knew that a 19-year-old student would be unsettled by such a professional appearance.

Each of them asked several questions of me, and the one I distinctly remember concerned my personal ambitions. The question was simply, "What are some of your goals?" I told them I wanted to finish college, give back to my community, and most importantly, build a better relationship with God. Though hesitant to speak of my spirituality, I had to be honest while sitting before the police—didn't want to risk being arrested for lying to the police.

At the completion of the meeting, one of the interviewers said they were impressed by all of my answers, including the one about my spirituality. This is what a maverick is all about—being yourself and making tough, independent decisions that may be unpopular to some, but you know they're right for you.

Within a couple of days, Lieutenant Blair called to notify me of my acceptance in the summer internship program with the Cleveland Metroparks Ranger Department. I understood her to be a very professional businesswoman—as serious as serious gets!

Consequently, I didn't express my excitement when I received her call, as I was concerned she would consider me immature and withdraw the offer. So I waited patiently until we finished our phone conversation to run upstairs and tell my mom the good news. My mother was proud and very encouraging. I told her how much I feared Lieutenant Blair, and she told me, "Well welcome to the "real world," Antoine."

I had to complete the student orientation process before beginning the internship and this is where I learned that two other students were also selected. One attended high school with me, and the other kid was from a different school. None of us really knew what to expect, but we were happy to have an internship that paid $8.00 an hour, when minimum wage was $5.15. And after the orientation process, we reported to the Ranger Department's Headquarters and were introduced to many of the staff members and rangers.

The Internship Begins
There are over ten parks in the Cleveland Metroparks' system, which allowed my fellow interns and I permanent assignment to park zones that were relatively close to our residencies. However, to broaden our exposure, we often traveled to various parks. It was a must to have a vehicle because some parks are located in remote areas, in compari-

son to the inner-city where I lived. It was actually kind of fun visiting different parks because it helped me become familiar with other areas and communities within my region.

Working with the Ranger Department was predominantly a shadowing experience, as I was able to directly participate only in a limited number of activities. Keep in mind, I was interning with police officers who were on the beats in the streets. They couldn't put me in harm's way by allowing me to perform arrests, or interact with aggressive criminals. Without compromising my safety, the rangers were still able to make the internship fun and beneficial for me.

The goal of the program was to ensure that the other interns and I were exposed to the many facets of the Ranger Department. One way the department achieved this goal was by requiring each of us to spend time with all of its operational units. And I made certain to keep a journal so I could remember all of my experiences.

The first field experience I recall was with the Mounted Unit. While spending a few days at the stable I learned about the patrol process via horse, and the importance of utilizing horses, especially for crowd control or canvassing wooded areas. I also had the opportunity to groom and clean the horses, which is part of a daily routine for the stable workers. But darn—I didn't have the opportunity to actually ride the horses, due to a liability issue more than anything. Nevertheless, it was fascinating to learn that law enforcement horses fill a need greater than simply prancing in public parades.

I learned next, from the Enforcement Unit. Their duties are to handle special operations cases. For example, these rangers are responsible for securing the zoo, and at one point the parking lots were experiencing stolen car problems. As a result, this particular unit set up a sting operation and dressed as normal zoo visitors. Officers circulated throughout the large parking lot areas and even surveilled from building tops. I didn't do much with this squad besides some behind-the-scenes planning, for such sting operations.

The Enforcement Unit also often tagged up with the Traffic Unit to help slow motor vehicle drivers down by creating speed zones and issuing traffic tickets when necessary. I enjoyed riding with officers when they wrote traffic violations because sometimes I watched for speeders by monitoring the radar meter, and was alert for other illegal traffic infractions. I also used my discretion and advised the ranger which car he or she should pull over for a violation—this made me feel like I was really part of the ranger team.

My advice to you (if you're pulled over by an officer) is to be truthful, respectful, and nicely ask for a warning. The worst he or she can tell you is no, so it's worth a shot; you might be surprised what you can get in life if you just ask!

Another fun experience was working with the Bicycle Unit. A certified law enforcement bike trainer shared techniques with me about how to operate a bike as a law enforcement tool. As you may imagine, bikes are used to travel through wooded areas and other places in the park that are relatively inaccessible by car. Rangers need to be in good shape because they respond to calls that often require riding the bike to a specific scene, or back to the patrol vehicle. Both of these destinations can be a very uncomfortable trip when cycling as fast as you can in an emergency situation.

In one instance, a ranger and I left the squad car and rode our bicycles down a hill. As soon as we reached the bottom, we noticed a vehicle speeding up the hill. So guess what we had to do? Since the officer abruptly decided to catch this individual, we had to turn around and cycle back up the hill to the squad car. The ranger was definitely in much better shape than me because he was far ahead, on our way back up that hill. I can still hear him shouting, "Come on man … hurry up!"

Now, I'm not a quitter by any means, but I tell you what, I almost gave up on that pursuit and was very close to telling him to go ahead without me! I wasn't sure I would make it back up that hill fast enough. However, to my surprise, I eventually made it. We hopped in the vehicle to give pursuit, but of course the man was long gone by then. What a wasteful workout!

The Dive Unit was another area I learned from during training sessions at a remote beach location. While at the beach, rangers simulated real life scenarios by submerging various objects into the water. After donning their necessary equipment, they dove into the water to search for various objects that were submerged for training purposes. Usually, they returned to shore with the intended objects in hand. This training was generally an all day event and even more fun because they barbecued for lunch.

But the K-9 Unit was my absolute favorite. It felt like I was the cameraman for the popular *Cops* television show because like the member of a camera crew, all I could do was watch and soak in the exciting, action-filled experience. Officers working in the K-9 Unit typically stopped drivers for a traffic violation and proceeded to search the vehicle for drugs or other illegal items.

Another tip for you—officers typically can't search your car without your permission, unless they specifically see something illegal, in plain sight, or detect a drug, like the smell of marijuana. Of course many citizens don't know this and simply comply when officers ask to search their vehicle. I witnessed a lot of instances when the officer discovered self-incriminating evidence in the car, only because the owner gave consent to search when they weren't legally obligated to do so.

Radar was the name of the police dog that belonged to the Ranger Department. Radar knew his job, and did it well. It was so fascinating to see how Radar sniffed a car and would be so effective at locating where drugs were in the car. He would walk around the targeted car several times and begin to eagerly scratch and bark in the direction of an area, if he located any drugs.

After incriminating evidence was discovered by the ranger, it was fascinating to witness how two individuals would be separated during questioning and one person would snitch on the other about the craziest things. Usually the stories were contradictory, but the officer almost always ultimately discovered the truth. People lied, cried, and gave terribly lame excuses. All I can say is just imagine being the cameraman on *Cops*, and you will have a feel for how much fun it was.

Another of my choice assignments was directing traffic when popular events created a lot of traffic in the parks. You may think I'm crazy for enjoying standing in the sun for hours while regulating the direction of traffic flow. In a sense, you are right to think that, but the only reason I absolutely loved it was because I had *authority*. Most often as an intern you don't have this.

When I say *authority*, I mean when I pointed at a car and authoritatively said stop, they stopped! When I directed them to go, they followed my instructions. When I yelled at them and told them to back up, they backed up! Though I took the responsibility seriously, it was tons of fun waving those colorful wands and blowing that annoying whistle—and the drivers had no choice but to respect my *authority*!

Working at the Cleveland Metroparks Zoo was another terrific experience, mostly because I enjoyed interacting with the public and seeing family and friends who visited the zoo. While patrolling the zoo, I drove a golf cart and was equipped with a radio that allowed me to communicate with the rangers on duty.

Since the golf cart had a ranger emblem on it, many people thought I was an actual ranger. Because a zoo trip usually entails a lot of walking, often, someone would jokingly (but sometimes seriously) offer me money to take them from one place to another. Of course I never did this, but the attention was great!

It was also rewarding when some people had questions and addressed me as "sir" or "officer." What an awesome experience for a young college student, who knew he was an intern, but enjoyed being addressed as "police officer."

Speaking of police officer, I even did one little short undercover operation in one of the parks I was assigned to. I remember working with one ranger who took advantage of my civilian clothes.[9] One evening while on the beat, we suspected that a group of teenagers (sitting around a picnic table) were smoking marijuana. We hid behind some trees and he gave me orders to walk by the teens as if I was a regular park patron, and discretely flicker my flashlight once if it wasn't marijuana, and twice, if it was.

There was no doubt. I smelled the pungent herb and once I was past the table, I flickered my light twice. I hid my flashlight and walked back to the table so I could make small talk and distract them. The ranger crept up from behind without giving them a chance to hide the marijuana. He played it off as if he thought I was just an innocent bystander and told me to leave the area since I wasn't smoking anything—they were pissed, lol!

It's important to note that the officer expertly assessed the situation before I did this little undercover tactic to make certain it was safe to follow through. It wasn't risky because I just walked by as if I was taking a quiet evening walk in the park as an ordinary park patron.

From all of these experiences, there are many fascinating stories that I tell when talking to students about my educational and fun internship experiences. They get a thrill from them by living vicariously through me and my live, adrenaline rushing cop experiences.

---

[9] I dressed in civilian clothes instead of a ranger uniform while I was patrolling with the rangers.

Problems I Encountered and How I Handled Them

Rejection by other employees—Initially, coming through the door as an intern, I wasn't fully accepted by some. One reason is because my hair was in braids, and some of the rangers thought that I didn't maintain a professional appearance by wearing braids. The first time I learned someone had a problem with my hairstyle was when some rangers and I were talking about golf. One ranger said, "Yeah, Antoine can come out and golf with us when he cuts those braids off."

Thank God for Lieutenant Blair. She went to bat for me on many occasions, and this was one of them. She was a part of the conversation and asked me to close the door to the room we were in, as she began to emphatically scold and explain to the others that it was okay for me to have braids. She indicated to them that I was not a ranger, but a college student, who had the right to wear braids.

Now, I could have spoken my mind and fired back at those guys rather than allowing Lieutenant Blair to protect me. I could have told them to give me a chance and not to judge a book by a stereotypical cover. But I had to keep in mind that I *was* an intern, and I had to take the criticism (within reason).

However, I learned from this incident that most internship supervisors value you as an intern, and will fight for you when necessary—as long as you are not in the wrong. If I would have openly expressed my discontent with the gentlemen, I might have put myself in a terrible situation because regular employees essentially can make or break your internship experience. By not sharing good information with you or even worse, allowing you to do something during your experience that they know will get you in trouble with your boss, full-time workers may choose to sabotage your experience—don't give them a reason while *Interning CEO Style.*

Instant Messaging trouble—One weekend I was working out of the Headquarters office and it was almost time to leave for the day—but I had to find something to kill that last half-hour of my shift. While sitting at a computer, I decided to go online and download some software for Instant Messenger. After maybe a week or so, Lieutenant Blair came to me and asked if I or any of the other interns had done something to one of the computers. I had forgotten about the Instant Messenger download, and told her that it wasn't me. She asked a couple more times, and I finally thought to tell her it may have been the software I installed on the computer.

She kindly explained to me the importance of not doing that type of activity on a company or organization's equipment without permission. This is a perfect situation to illustrate how an employee could allow an intern to fail. Although it didn't actually happen, a full-time employee could have been aware that I downloaded an Instant Messenger application. Or even perhaps watched me do it, knowing I would get into trouble by the supervisor.

What a lesson for discussing personal problems during an internship—It's vitally important for you to be careful what you discuss with others at your internship. Unfortunately, I had to learn this the hard way. Several months before the internship began, someone had stolen my identity and opened a cellular phone account with my personal information. Of course, they ran the bill up and the creditors came after me.

Since I was interning with a law enforcement agency, I thought it was a good idea to ask for advice on how to proceed with this issue. However, apparently while explaining my situation to a ranger who was in management, I gave the wrong impression. This person somehow thought I was falsifying everything I told them. I became terribly offended.

They thought I was acting irresponsibly and *I* was the person who caused the phone bill to become extremely high, and was simply trying to get out of paying the bill. This of course, was not the case, as I was merely an innocent victim of fraud.

I learned from this situation that some personal comments are better left unsaid, especially when trying to build a positive intern image in the professional environment. Be careful what you speak or discuss during your internship, as misperceived statements can distort your image.

The importance of an intern's professional appearance and attire—On a couple of occasions, Lieutenant Blair noticed that I periodically reported to work wearing wrinkled clothes. On other days, my hands were ashy because I had forgotten to put on lotion. Even though I thought she was extremely hard on me at times, she never confronted me about a situation in front of others. She always pulled me to the side and counseled me about the problem, though rather candidly.

This proved to be very helpful and I later appreciated her methods; she didn't have to do things in such a considerate manner. In my years of interning, I've noticed that some interns arrive to work with a sloppy, wrinkled, or unclean appearance. As a result, they often lose credibility with their coworkers and employers, simply because they don't take care to dress in an appropriate fashion.

It's also important to note that many internship supervisors will not take the extra time to explain the importance of the fundamentals of professionalism to interns, so make certain your grooming and appearance are always superior. Dressing nicely is also a psychological thing. For me, when I dress nicely at my internship, it makes me feel more like I'm part of the team. Actually, if you work in a medium to large internship people may mistake you for someone who is an established employee—this shouldn't be you.

A lesson about arriving late to work—As I mentioned before, some parks to which I was assigned were relatively far from my home. To account for arrival time, rangers and interns reported to the dispatch center over the radio frequency that we were "in-service" at the start of each shift. This meant that everyone on duty knew the exact time that each employee began their work shift. Lieutenant Blair's policy for interns allowed up to three late arrivals, after which they were automatically dismissed from the internship program.

I took this rule lightly, because as a talented athlete in high school, I was always able to get out of trouble. It's true, leniency for athletes was commonplace. However, during my first summer internship here, I received a rude awakening. It wasn't until my second late day that I realized Lieutenant Blair's tardy policy was not a game. At this point, she spoke privately to me and explained gravely that I would be fired the next time I arrived late to work.

I told her I had between a 40-60 minute commute to work and often had to fight traffic. After stating this, I asked what time she suggested I leave my home in order for me to arrive to work by 7:00 a.m. Her explicit reply was, "I don't care if you leave your house at 6:59 a.m., just make sure you get to work by 7:00 a.m." I thought that was rather harsh for an intern to hear, but again this was the "real world."

So of course, me being young and inexperienced, I was on my way to arriving late that third time and fired as a result. Traveling along the express highway to work, I was cruising to my loud music. I looked in my rearview mirror and saw the colors of the American flag. Only these colors didn't represent independence or liberty; instead, they were flashing lights on top of an Ohio State Highway Patrol's police cruiser—uh-oh, I was being pulled over by a cop. And the part that really sucked was that I was only five minutes away from work!

The police officer approached my car and I handed over my driver's license. In hopes of getting off the hook, I told him I was an intern with the Metroparks Ranger Department. He said, "And ... what are you telling me for?!"

I responded eloquently with, "Uh, uh ... oh, I'm sorry." After learning that I was an intern with a law enforcement agency, I truly thought he would let me leave, immediately so I could make it to work on time! Obviously, I was terribly incorrect with my assumption.

He walked back to his cruiser and returned shortly, asking me to turn the vehicle off and step out of the car so I could be patted down. As I stepped out of the vehicle the patrolman looked at his partner, who had just arrived on the scene, and yelled to him, "We got us another one!" (He was referring to a careless driver that was about to be cited for speeding.)

The officer's stern demeanor I really thought I was doomed after hearing the police officer's exclamation. And since he noticed that the license plate stickers on my vehicle were expired, he indicated that I couldn't drive the car home. He instructed me to have the vehicle towed back to my house.

reminded me a lot of Lieutenant Blair, and I thought they both were conspiring against me because he appeared to be extremely inflexible and about his business. I was ushered into the back of the police cruiser, feeling terrible, as if I had let my family down. Shortly thereafter, he began to drive, with me scrunched in the back seat of his cruiser. During this miserable ride, I tried to think about how I would explain to my mom—not only did I lose my job, but I was also in jail!

I was certain he was driving me to the police station, but I began to recognize some of the streets he was taking, which were in the direction of the park I was assigned to for that day. If I had a million dollars to bet on something, I would have never bet that he would give me a break because it appeared as if he had no sympathy for me.

I kept mute, as the officer was actually *speeding* to get me to work on time! Once we arrived at the ranger's office I was certain the officer was going to speak with the ranger I was shadowing, to let him know I had been stopped for speeding. But he didn't. I hopped out of the cruiser and silently thanked the Lord that everything worked out okay from this incident.

In short, always be on time for your internship, and don't speed on purpose, in hopes of getting pulled over so a cop can give you a speedy ride to get you there on time. My instance was a result of nothing but pure serendipity!

Receiving Helpful Guidance from the Rangers

The first summer I interned with the Ranger Department there were three interns. However, I was the only one who returned for the following summer internship program. I wasn't sure why the other two interns didn't return, as well, but I was happy that the Ranger Department was impressed enough with this *CEO Style Intern* to warrant my return.

My two summer internship with the Ranger Department afforded me the opportunity to work and ride along with a variety of rangers. They were a diverse group of professionals with unique backgrounds. This "real world" exposure was great, as it enabled me to participate in intimate and candid conversations with them about career and professional guidance. They were all willing to answer my questions and offer different perspectives on all of my curious inquiries.

This was very different than talking to my peers or professors. I was actually in the "real world," working behind the scenes with real professionals, rather than reading a textbook about the life of a police officer. Once again, these types of experiences are invaluable because you are able to take some of this information back to the classroom and use it in a discussion or to complete an assignment.

While *Interning CEO Style*, take advantage of your time at your internship and utilize its many resources. Most professionals enjoy talking to interns and giving them advice because they have already been down the paths we're taking; therefore, they understand the importance of helping students as much as they can.

Many times people asked if I wanted to become a ranger once I finished college, and I typically answered with a general response. During these internship experiences some rangers explained that when others ask about my ambitions, to never quickly dismiss a career as a ranger. It was explained to me that some full-time employees do not see the need to invest in an intern who does not have the desire to work for that respective organization. So their advice was to express to others that I was exploring the ranger profession, though not completely sure what I wanted to do just yet.

To this end, I always shared with them that becoming a ranger was something I was receptive to. This was true for me, and it's an appropriate answer for you to give when someone asks you this question during your internship. Internships are useful tools for navigating a career to determine your true passions. Most supervisors will respect the fact that you are young and open to new ideas and experiences; they understand that you may not have your career plans totally mapped out.

As a result of my receptiveness to the Ranger Department, I met many professionals and was exposed to the criminal justice arena by working behind the scenes as an intern. It was with the Ranger Department where I learned the basics about workplace politics, punctuality, and appearance in the professional world. Later in my internship career I noticed that numerous interns, who were college seniors, still didn't understand the importance of these three aspects. I'm grateful for Lieutenant Blair and her dedication to professionalism, which helped me write this chapter of internship advice for you.

To show my appreciation, I actually met with Lieutenant Blair for lunch a few years after my internships with the Ranger Department. During this time I asked her if she was really going to fire me if I had been late that third time. Can you believe she said yes that she was going to seriously fire me!? She explained that she probably would have allowed me to come back the following summer, though. However, she felt that it was vital for me to learn the importance of reporting to work on time because many companies fire people on the spot when underperforming, or consistently arriving late.

To this day, I'm actually a stickler for promptness to everything, whether it's work or playing basketball with friends. This value pays off and many professionals have complimented me on my punctuality. Being on time shows you aren't selfish and are considerate of other people's time. It's something you should practice everyday as *a CEO Style Intern.*

In conclusion, as the two quotes at the beginning of this chapter suggest, never be afraid or doubt your abilities because you're young and inexperienced. Instead, believe in your natural and learned abilities to obtain success in the intimidating "real world," so you can become a light to your internship organization.

Intern CEO Style
Leadership Principles

> **Prepare for your interview.** Just because you are young and inexperienced, don't be afraid of an intimidating "real world" interview setting. A lot of preparation can help you overcome this anxiety.

> **Dress professionally.** To *Intern CEO Style*, you must dress and present yourself like a CEO. Dress to impress at your internship, but don't go overboard. Observe what others are wearing and ask your supervisor for advice about the most appropriate attire. Also, many jobs allow its employees to dress casually on Fridays. Monitor your coworkers' dress style on these days to determine what type of attire is appropriate for Fridays.

> **Chronicle your experiences.** Whether it is required or not, keep a journal and take notes on everything you do. This will help you remember what you've learned as an intern. You should also create a portfolio that includes all of your projects and assignments. Put these documents in a binder so they will be organized because you may want to take this to future interviews, to highlight your past experiences. However, allow your current internship supervisor to review the portfolio to make certain you didn't include any private or confidential information.

> **Punctuality is a must—be on time.** Being late or tardy is completely unacceptable, so be on time. Better yet, make it a point to arrive between five and fifteen minutes early to work, meetings, and all other appointments.

> **Don't abuse a flexible work schedule.** Some internship organizations are flexible to the point where they allow interns to create their own work days and hours. With this flexibility, students may be able to change their work days and hours throughout their internship. If you have a flexible schedule, don't abuse or continuously change it.

For example, if you set up your schedule for Monday, Wednesday, and Friday from 9:00 a.m. to 5:00 p.m., don't change from this schedule often. Your colleagues will be depending on you to be consistent with your work schedule as much as possible. Use your flexibility to change your work schedule when you really need it, and it's up to you to determine what constitutes legitimate reasons for using your flexibility.

> **Always be honest about things, especially your time-sheet and office supplies.** Sometimes you will receive permission from your supervisor to alter your timesheet for the benefit of giving you extra time off to study for an exam, or take care of other personal business. However, never *ever* take it upon yourself to alter or fudge your timesheet by your own choice. Moreover, never steal or borrow anything without asking permission for the items. These are a very dishonest practices and could land you in tons of trouble, or even be grounds for terminating your internship. This reputation could follow you for many years down the road, and therefore your chances of getting future internships or full-time jobs would be negatively impacted.

> **Develop strong soft-social skills and work on becoming a "people person."** These skills will help you enjoy and appreciate working in a diverse workforce. Many people will be older than you and come from extremely different backgrounds, but your interpersonal skills should assist you in learning more about others and effectively working with them. You don't have to necessarily be friends with everyone, but you must know how to respectfully maintain healthy professional relationships.

> **Avoid coworker conflicts.** Don't argue with your colleagues or have an attitude if they don't readily accept you. If there's a problem, see your supervisor privately and immediately to resolve the issue. You can also confide in school representatives or your mentors for additional support, especially if the problem is with your boss. Don't discuss your conflicts with anyone at your internship unless you are convinced that you can trust them.

Misplaced trust could make the situation worse if they were to report your concerns to the problematic individuals, without your knowledge.

➤ **Never criticize or irritate your fellow coworkers.** In my internship experiences, I noticed that other interns would often challenge coworkers and supervisors. They asked difficult questions in hopes of baffling the person, to make them look stupid. In other instances, the intern would purposely irritate other coworkers and do simple things to upset them.

Examples of some of the things you shouldn't do are 1) Create attention in front of others to point out a co-worker's tardiness, 2) Fail to relay phone messages to others, and 3) Speak sarcastically to coworkers, or not speak to them at all.

➤ **Don't engage or get pulled into office politics.** Avoid gossip, maintain a positive energetic attitude, and don't compromise your integrity. You can ruin your image and reputation by engaging in unhealthy office politics, so don't do it.

➤ **Leave your personal problems at home.** Don't discuss personal affairs at work because others might misperceive your statements and make erroneous judgments about who you are.

➤ **Be inquisitive and ask questions.** Talk to the people in your internship organizations and ask intelligent questions. Seek their suggestions, tips, and advice that will prepare you for the "real world." Request their recommendations about how you can have a successful internship and career. Access to such professionals is a great resource for you, so use it. Also, doing this conveys your curiosity and interest in your internship responsibilities and the organization as a whole. It also helps you gain free knowledge.

➤ **Don't tell others that you have no desire to work for the organization you're interning with, when you graduate.** If you are not certain this particular place or field of work is of long-term interest to you, simply explain to them that you are exploring the professional arena, and may be open to an opportunity with them should it present itself when you graduate from college.

➤ **Don't tolerate sexual harassment.**[10] If you ever feel that you are being sexually harassed or placed in an uncomfortable situation, speak with your mentors, school officials, or family members about this for their guidance. They may recommend that you privately confide in your supervisor for them to resolve this unfortunate issue.

➤ **Be smart about dating.** Some organizations strictly prohibit dating on the internship. Others are more lenient and allow dating. However, be smart and careful about this. If you decide to date, I would strongly recommend it being someone close to your age. But my first recommendation is to not date at all, as most of these office romances usually turn out to be a disaster.

➤ **Be careful with online social networks.** Don't log on social networking sites, such as MySpace, Facebook, Instant Messenger, or Twitter while you are at work. In addition, do not download any type of software on the organization's computers unless you have permission. Don't ask to log on social networking sites or download software packages unless you feel comfortable in doing so, and have a truly convincing reason that explains why you need to have access to these products during internship hours.

You shouldn't have information or pictures posted on any of these accounts that you wouldn't want your employer to see. For some organizations, they use these social networks to scan and dismiss applicants who post crazy photos or unprofessional content on their personal pages. Also, don't post any derogatory statements about your current internship organization or its employees because you could be fired for such postings.

➤ **Absolutely no sleeping while you are at your internship.** No matter how boring your work is or a meeting may be, sleeping on the job is an absolute no-no! It's important for you to always stay awake and be attentive be-

---

[10] I didn't experience any sexual harassment cases, but I wanted to provide some information on this topic for you.

cause sleeping on the job is an easy way for you to diminish your credibility, or even get fired.

➤ **Find out if you can intern again.** Some internship organizations allow previous interns to come back for another complete or partial internship experience. An example of a partial experience would be interning with one of your previous organizations during your winter break from school. Interning again is an excellent way to stay in the pipeline and foot in the door.

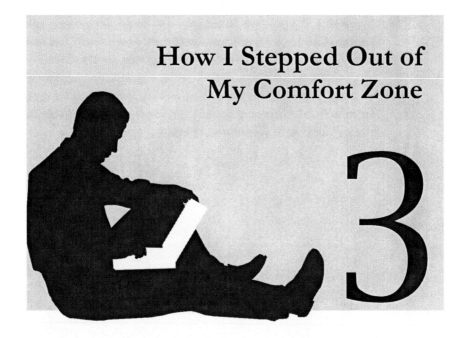

How I Stepped Out of My Comfort Zone

3

"Twenty years from now you will be more disappointed by the things you didn't do than by the ones you did do. So throw off the bowlines. Sail away from the safe harbor. Catch the trade winds in your sails. Explore. Dream. Discover."

Mark Twain

The Washington Semester Program—Spring 2004

This chapter highlights how I sailed away from my safe harbor and journeyed off into a very different world. It all began with a typical stack of junk mail. Maybe I was bored, but for some unknown reason I opened the packet of information from the Washington Semester Program at American University in Washington, D.C. and proceeded to read. It raised my eyebrows—in these days of numerous scams, it seemed *too good to be true*. This program was structured similar to a study abroad program, but students left their home college to live in D.C. rather another country.

At the time I applied, this program offered approximately 11 different fields for students to enroll in based upon a students' interests.

For example, I participated in the justice/law enforcement section of the program, since I had a passion for criminal justice.

This semester long experience was structured for students to attend seminar classes three days a week, to hear lectures from many experts or visit agencies in the criminal justice arena. For instance, my class toured the U.S. Supreme Court and received an educational lecture from Supreme Court Justice Ruth Bader Ginsburg. On the two remaining days of the week, we worked at an internship for eight hours a day.

Prior to arrival in D.C. and after acceptance into the Washington Semester Program, the accepted students allowed access to a huge database that contained information on hundreds of possible internships in the nation's capital city. The number of internships that were listed really made me examine my career interests and narrow my focus!

Although this Washington Semester Program wasn't supported by Harvard University, I found the participating students' goals, ambitions, and work ethics to be just as superior as those of Harvard students. The nation's top and most hardworking students participated in this program. Even international student-achiever Miss Colombia for 2003, Diana Mantilla, was a former student in the program with me.

Also, I had the distinct opportunity during this program to become really cool classmates with America Ferrera. She was in the internship program too, before she wowed TV audiences in her leading role on the trendy sitcom, *Ugly Betty*. Like America, many of the students who enroll in this program often become celebrities in their fields and further their education by attending law or graduate school, and then pursuing creative careers in the "real world."

The Power of Networking

Before I left to study in D.C., I accessed the program's internship database to get a feel for which internships interested me. It took hours of eye-opening research to narrow down the prospective internships, but equipped with data and enthusiasm, I set up a time to meet with a married couple—Steve and Linda, two of my most active mentors.

Armed with information on three of the internships that complemented my criminal justice background and one internship that was political in nature, I thought my future career was imminent.

Though I was primarily interested in law enforcement internships, my mentors felt it was time for me to step outside of my comfort zone. They thought I should experience the political heart of America and climb up Capitol Hill.

An internship on Capitol Hill was number four on my priority list, yet Steve and Linda persuasively encouraged me to apply for the position as my number one choice. Consequently, I made the appropriate calls to set up an interview date with the Congressional Office of Congresswoman Stephanie Tubbs Jones. Before the interview I contacted one of my old supervisors, Clarence, from my ACLU internship. He had moved from my home city of East Cleveland, Ohio, to D.C. I told him that I was moving into town for a semester, and we made plans to hang out upon my arrival.

While we were talking on the phone I explained to him that I was preparing to apply for an internship on Capitol Hill. He asked with which representative. When I told him Congresswoman Stephanie Tubbs Jones, he exclaimed that his best friend, Anthony, worked in her office and was probably the person who would be my interviewer. Clarence instructed me to add his name as a reference, so he could speak to Anthony on my excellent intern record while under his supervision at the ACLU; and that's exactly what I did.

To better prepare for the interview, I made a trip to Capitol Hill prior to my appointment—wouldn't want to get lost on the way to my interview! I also conducted some standard research on the Congresswoman and the district she represented, to familiarize myself with her typical politics and position on key issues.

Having close interactions with high-ranking politicians and their staff assistants were a totally new experience for me. Was I a little nervous on the day of the interview? Absolutely! However, just as any leader does when experiencing a natural level of anxiety while striving for success, I put my fears aside and approached the interview with an air of confidence.

Upon my arrival at the Congresswoman's office I learned that it was indeed, Anthony who was scheduled to conduct my interview. He asked questions that I effectively answered and a few others that I stumbled on because my natural interests were not in politics. At the conclusion of the interview he explained that the office already had enough interns. But the more we talked and the more he studied me, he soon indicated that he could make room for me if I was truly interested in acquiring this internship—I happily accepted the position!

This situation was very similar to Chapter One's recount of the ACLU's budget modification they made for me. To my understanding, there was funding for only 11 interns, but I was the last person they decided to hire during their application review process, so they had to adjust their budget accordingly.

This is what being marketable is all about: My resumé got me the interview, but the interview got me the job. During the Capitol Hill interview, I made certain to display my natural curiosity and outgoing personality by effectively highlighting my skills and experiences, while asking intelligent questions. Believe it or not, many people aren't good at this type of self-promotion during an interview. However, after reading *Learn to Intern CEO Style*, you should have the confidence to handle an interview well and make the employer *want you* to be part of their team.

Moreover, you may think that Clarence was partly the reason I was offered this internship on Capitol Hill—if so, you are right. What I had just experienced was *the power of networking. Networking* is simply meeting professionals and building positive relationships with them or just keeping their business cards on hand for future contact purposes. Networking works!

I made the conscious decision to keep in touch with Clarence over the years to create and maintain a healthy network. I kept him abreast of the progress in my life, especially with school and work. As a result, his networking and friendship with Anthony became an advantage for me. Of course Anthony didn't have to hire me, but Clarence probably called him before the interview and suggested I would be worth the investment. Nonetheless, I appreciate the fact that Anthony made an exception for me.

At the time I was interviewed for the internship I didn't know how powerful this experience would be for me. However, in hindsight, I think about how the benefits of this internship have, and are still, paying off. It was the foundation for my future experiences because it exposed me to so many different fields. Through that exposure, I became equipped with the skills and confidence needed to apply for future internships outside of my comfort zone.

My Internship on Capitol Hill in Washington, D.C., with the Office of Congresswoman Stephanie Tubbs Jones

The basic structure of this internship was:

Hands-on	Part-time—Spring semester
Unpaid	Multiple interns
Out of town	No paid tuition
Instructor supervision	No job offer
Academic Credit	

Life as a Congressional Intern

Capitol Hill is an incredible place to work because this prestigious site is the heart and soul of our American government. The Capitol building is made of brick clad in marble and sandstone that stretches to be more than 751 feet tall and 350 feet wide. The caste-iron statue that rests on top of the Capitol building's dome is 19 feet and six inches tall, and named as the Statue of Freedom.

Comprised of the House and Senate Chambers, these two branches of Congress employ thousands of professionals and interns. I am pleased and fortunate to have been included as one.

On my first day I walked up the plethora of steps to the Capitol building donning the finest suit I had in my wardrobe—ready to tackle the world. But I didn't know that my first day was going to take me for a stressful ride. I was overwhelmed when I first arrived, and the training caused an information overload. Learning how to conduct legislative research, write memos, and respond to constituents' concerns in the form of letters, emails and phone calls, was just the beginning.

I was also trained to give tours of Capitol Hill for visiting constituents from the 11th Congressional District of Ohio. Although this was a wonderful experience, it represented a challenge, as I was expected to know most of the history that pertained to Capitol Hill. All of this intense training paid off because I was soon able to effectively network and interact with some inquisitive and intelligent constituents while giving tours.

In order for me to be successful in responding to the concerns of the constituents that were often expressed through letters and emails, I had the pleasurable task of reading Cleveland's local and other national newspapers, on a daily basis. By keeping up with what was going on in the city and around the country, I was more valuable to the constituents and their questions. I also conducted more extensive research on issues that were unfamiliar to me in order to respond effectively on behalf of the Congresswoman. This process helped me become acquainted with many topics outside of my preferred field of criminal justice; I was exposed to environmental, healthcare, and tax issues.

Specific to the Congresswoman's responsibilities in office, I prepared some materials for the Congresswoman to present on the House floor. One memorable opportunity was my preparation of a tribute to Cleveland native, Garrett Morgan, a gifted inventor; it was printed in the Congressional Record and read by the Congresswoman on the House floor, in recognition of Black History Month.

In addition, this internship allowed me to be involved with public outreach initiatives; as an example, I participated in a reading lunch program that the Congresswoman supported. Every other Monday my immediate supervisor and I took turns visiting a local school to mentor and tutor various students during our lunch break. What a rewarding experience!

This Capitol Hill internship provided me with many advantages, and one of my favorites was the opportunity to attend live briefings and hearings on complex issues, such as Homeland Security. These activities can often be viewed on CSPAN or other news stations, but seeing them live is a vivid reminder of the kind of power and influence that congressional representatives possess.

On most occasions when my co-interns and I supported the Congresswoman at these types of events, she made certain to introduce us to the audience. It was a wonderful benefit for us because after these sessions people would often converse and treat us with professional respect due to our association with the Congresswoman—this definitely made me feel like I was *Interning CEO Style!*

Socializing and Networking with Celebrities on the Hill
Capitol Hill is where all of the federal legislation is debated and created. Numerous citizens visit this institution on a daily basis to meet with their representatives or attend functions that are open to the public. Many of these functions are social in nature and take place after work hours, in the form of a reception. It was a privilege for

instance, for me to attend a voter registration initiative sponsored by professional wrestler, Kurt Angle.

On another occasion while working and listening to the television that was stationed on CNN, the reporter spoke about Capitol Hill. He announced that Michael Jackson was there to meet with Congressman Chaka Fattah.

It was a routine workday, yet I kind of felt like I was at home in East Cleveland, Ohio, listening to the news like the rest of the nation. But incredibly, I wasn't at home—I was on Capitol Hill. Wow! This meant I could actually go *see* Michael Jackson during his visit—and I did just that.

The news reporter indicated that Jackson would be in the Rayburn House Office Building, so I quickly walked over, and of course, there were people lined up on both sides of the hallway. Michael Jackson walked by giving the peace sign as a greeting. I distinctly recall a couple of young ladies literally crying because they were so surprised and happy to actually see the "King of Pop."

Capitol Hill was never dull. Once, as I prepared to leave for the day, the Congresswoman asked me if I had anything to do after work. Now, we all know that's a leading question ... even though I did, I told her I didn't have anything planned for the evening. She was pleased and asked if I wanted to "go on a date" with her to meet a new, young representative who was planning to run for a seat in the Senate Chamber of Congress. Of course, it was intimidating because I was one-on-one with the Congresswoman while walking the halls of America's political powerhouse.

The Congresswoman decided that we would hop on the underground subway train that serves as a shuttle service for members of Congress and their staff. This subway system is a transportation service that can be used to avoid the long walk between the House and Senate Chambers.

When leaving the House of Representatives to enter the Senate, people must generally wait in lines to be searched by security; but not this *CEO Style Intern* because that day, I was a VIP. Since I was with the Congresswoman, I was able to avoid the long security checkpoints. My favorite phrase that was directed towards security officials and members of Congress was, "He's with me." When she pronounced these words, I too, was treated like a member of royal Congress.

There were several other representatives already socializing when we arrived at the function. They were speaking to this new, young gentleman who planned to run for office. At the conclusion of the session someone asked me to take a picture of the group. I kindly took the camera and snapped a few pictures for the representatives, with Senator Barack Obama standing in the middle of the group. Yes, the new young Senator-to-be progressed to become President Obama. I had the opportunity to meet and mingle with the future President of the United States back in 2004, when few people knew how far his ambitions would take him.

Before the conclusion of this internship I made certain to speak personally with all of the legislative aides in the office of Congresswoman Tubbs Jones. I asked for their tips and advice on how to ensure a successful future. They offered suggestions such as "read everything," "don't be afraid of new experiences," "maintain a journal during internships," "create a portfolio that highlights your achievements," "be receptive," and last but not least, "be true to yourself and what you stand for."

The last person I met with was the Congresswoman. She asked about my interests after leaving her office. I explained that I had a desire to become an FBI agent. She told me she would write a letter to the FBI's Cleveland field office on my behalf, and suggested I pursue an internship with them. As a result of this formal networking encounter, I guess it's no big surprise that the next chapter is about my internship with the FBI.

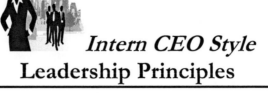

Intern CEO Style
Leadership Principles

> **Broaden your career horizons.** When putting Mark Twain's quote in the context of internships you should, "Sail away from your safe harbor and explore, dream, and discover" your career path by taking advantage of internships.

> **Relocate if you can.** Take advantage of an internship that requires you to relocate to a different city, state, or country. With this adventure, you will become familiar with another area and observe a wider variety of people and organizations, outside of your comfort zone.

> **Pursue unpaid internships.** Unpaid internships are still valuable even though you're not receiving monetary compensation, as they often lead to future paid internships and full-time jobs.

> **Thoroughly research the organization you are applying to.** Review the organization's history, goals, and mission statement before the interview. Talk about these aspects and how your skills align with them during the interview meeting.

> **Know where you're going for your interview.** Some time prior to the interview, ride or walk by the building in which your interview will be held, so you will know exactly where you are going and how long it will take for you to get there.

> **Make yourself available to the staff.** Help as much as you can with projects or assignments that may require your assistance. If you don't have a lot of responsibilities, be proactive and ask staff members if they need any extra help.

> **Build positive relationships by expressing gratitude and appreciation to the staff.** Periodically, demonstrate your appreciation for the staff members taking the time

to work with and help develop you. Expressing gratitude conveys that you are thankful and unselfish.

> **Know that networking is vital to your success.** Someone once said, "It's not always who you know. But, it's also about who knows you, too." Network to attain your first internship. Network for your next internship. And then ultimately network to attract job offers. Use internship colleagues and supervisors as resources to prepare for your next internship experience or job.

> **Accept social event invitations.** Whether it's on or off the clock, accept invitations to hang out with your boss, or even other full-time employees as much as possible. Do this only if you are comfortable with the setting of the event. You will meet many resourceful people this way; it also offers you the opportunity to hold intimate conversations and build more enduring relationships.

> **Participate in social activities that happen around the office.** If you notice that every Friday someone brings in doughnuts, talk to someone and find out if you can participate as a Friday doughnut provider. Or if you notice that every so often someone brings in some type of treat for the office, jump right in and bring a treat a time or two. Also, if you are given the opportunity to sit on the planning committee for a holiday party, do it. Doing these types of things show that you are a team player and enjoy being part of the organization.

> **Learn proper meal etiquette.**[11] This is extremely important to practice when you accept social event invitations. Learn how to properly use your silverware and carry-on an informal professional conversation.

> **Never end your internship on a bad note.** Completing your internship in good standing is essential because you never know if you will need help or support from someone within that organization in the future.

---

[11] You can do an Internet search for meal and conversation etiquette tips, if you need specific guidance on this topic.

How I Gained Lasting Respect from My Family, Peers, and Community that FBI Special Agents Receive

4

"Superstars who don't want the responsibility that comes with public acclaim don't have that choice. They are role models whether they like it or not; they cannot simply announce that they intend to shirk their responsibility. They are role models, either good or bad. So are you. So am I. I believe we have an obligation to make that model a positive one."[12]

John Wooden

My Humbling and Rocky Experiences during the FBI Application Process

Although I was accepted into an internship on Capitol Hill, I was still skeptical about my ability to literally achieve whatever I put my mind to. I still didn't necessarily believe I would be able to obtain an internship with the Federal Bureau of Investigation (FBI).

[12] Reprinted with permission of The McGraw-Hill Companies. *Wooden: A Lifetime of Observations and Reflections On and Off the Court.* Copyright © 1997 by Coach John Wooden with Steve Jamison.

One reason was because this was my dream job—and I never thought I would actually have an opportunity to work behind the scenes with my *dream* job. The second reason was because this was the "FBI" we were talking about! As you know, FBI agents are featured in many fascinating television shows that glorify their intriguing work. I never imagined I would have the privilege of being exposed to all of this media-captivating action.

Nonetheless, after speaking with Congresswoman Stephanie Tubbs Jones about my potential ideal career, I began to investigate the FBI's internship process. I called the Cleveland field office and requested information about their internship program. One of the program's standards was that students must have a cumulative grade point average of a 3.0—but I only had a 2.9. I still believed, however, I was a competitive candidate. I knew it would be hard work to get accepted into this program, but I didn't want to settle for less than what I truly wanted.

I developed a phrase out of the word S.E.T.T.L.E.—*Something Else That Takes Little Effort*. And with this internship, I was not going to settle for *Something Else That Took Little Effort!* Instead, I reached for the stars by giving it as much effort as I reasonably could in order to be accepted into the FBI's internship program.

I applied approximately nine months before the internship was scheduled to begin because I was aware that the process would be very long and thorough.

So extensive were the procedures, it felt like I was applying for an actual FBI special agent position. I had to complete a form that required me to list information about myself for the last ten years from the date when I applied for the internship. To put this in perspective for you, I was mandated to provide historical information that transpired between 1995 and 2005, which included *every single* one of my previous work experiences and residencies. Since I had many part-time jobs and different addresses within that timeframe, this was painful as it tested my recollection of many exact dates!

In addition to the complicated and frustrating paperwork, the FBI conducted a rigorous background check on me. All of the people I listed as references called and told me they were nervous when they answered their phone and heard five distinct words, "Hello. This is the FBI." Initially, my references thought the FBI was investigating them until the special agents explained the nature of the call—both humor and panic wrapped up in five simple words! I got a kick out of this because these innocent individuals were nervous, as if they were about to go to jail. Lol.

Another funny story I recall is the day when special agents walked around my college campus, Baldwin-Wallace College, and randomly asked people if they were familiar with me. At first I thought, why would they waste their time? What's the possibility of finding many (if any) students on a large college campus that would know one particular person?

I became aware of this investigatory tactic when a friend of mine told me they questioned her while she walked to class. I was shocked! However, I suppose their perception was if I were a trouble-causing student, or less than superior in character, then more people would know of me, and offer unfavorable testimonies. And likewise the case if I was a stand-out, exemplary student, they would speak highly of me.

Delving further into my campus persona, the FBI agents were on my college's campus completing my background check on a day my roommate, Nick, decided to play his X-Box after taking a shower. While playing the video game, he heard a few knocks on the door. Without getting up, he verbally welcomed the visitor in with a shout through the door.

The agents knocked again—and again, Nick shouted for them to open the door. Still, no one appeared in the doorway. So he stormed to the door, with a bath towel around his waist, swung it open and yelled, "I *said* come in!"

Before he knew it a gold badge appeared followed by the infamous words, "FBI"—I can only imagine the look of shock on his face. He explained to me that his heart dropped his stomach—and of course, that he quickly changed his rude demeanor. Lol.

This was actually pretty spooky because how could they possibly know I wasn't in the room? In fact, I generally would be in my room during that time on a regular day. Nevertheless, I found it to be hilarious hearing my roommate nervously relay this story, and to this day it still makes me laugh.

The application process also included an interview with a special agent. This was another awakening experience, as this would be my first one-on-one interaction with a special agent. Upon first walking into his office for the interview, it didn't help my nerves to hear his first words, "Mr. Moss, I see you have a record going on here ... "

I immediately thought to myself that he was reviewing the wrong file. I had never been in trouble before (with the law, at least). So I respectfully responded that I was afraid he was mistaking my records for another person's.

However, the thorough FBI profile on me referred to a couple of traffic tickets I received several years prior, as a high school student. I immediately thought about the ticket I received that I described in the chapter about my Cleveland Metroparks Ranger internship. I explained to him that I resolved those tickets and was informed by the license bureau that this history would be removed. He calmly replied, "This is the FBI and we can get any information we want, whether it's expunged or not." Hearing this was a huge wake up call, and this encounter helped me to be a more responsible citizen from that day forward.

Several days after I finished the interview, the FBI agent contacted me to inform me that I had advanced to the final stage of the application process—the polygraph examination. The polygraph test (lie detector test) was by far the most intimidating part of the investigation period that experienced, to become an FBI intern. As I was literally strapped to a chair, the examiner drilled me with a series of questions. He asked questions about my academic honesty in college, illegal drug interaction, and of course, my criminal history. After I completed the questions, the special agent walked into an isolated room to review the results that were being printed out by a machine.

He returned with a very stern look on his face and told me that the computer didn't like some of my responses. I must say, I was insulted! He dwelled on the questions that particularly pertained to drugs. I'm not sure if my results actually showed inconsistencies in my answers, or if I answered them okay and he thought I somehow beat the system. But it bothered me tremendously because I had never sold or used drugs a day in my life. Nonetheless, I went on to finish the test.

Finally—finishing the polygraph examination meant that I had completed the entire application process for the internship. Now all I had to do was wait to be contacted by the FBI after they rigorously analyzed my application, investigation reports, and polygraph results. I waited … and waited … until one day coming out of a class, I stopped by my dorm room to check my voicemail messages. There were several messages, but the only one I clearly remember today is an FBI representative saying, "Antoine, we would like to congratulate you for being accepted into the FBI internship program for the spring semester of 2005." I was so overjoyed and relieved, I began to thank God! I couldn't believe it. I was accepted for my *dream* internship with the FBI! But wait, my excitement however, was temporary.

After hearing the news of my acceptance into the program, I decided to speak with the college director of the Criminal Justice Department to share the great news with him. My plan was to ask him if he would be willing to serve as the college instructor who supervised my experience, so I could earn college credit.

I cheerfully divulged my news, and he quickly rejected my acceptance into the FBI internship program! He severely admonished me for not following college procedures when I applied for the internship; and since I attained the internship on my own without first consulting with him, he vehemently stated that I would not be able to intern with the FBI.

I told him I had already secured the position and didn't know that I had to speak with him before pursuing an internship position—but he *literally* yelled that he would call and tell them I was not qualified for the internship program. Feeling my future slipping away, I yelled back at him that I *really* wanted this internship because it was my dream job. However, he remained stern and we ended on the assumption that he would cancel my FBI internship.

I left his office in much pain while carrying a great deal of resentment towards this professor because he had appeared to strip away my dream internship position for an invalid reason. Even though he was the academic professional and initiated the yelling match, I regretted my lack of self-control that caused me to scream back at him. I thought about the cliché, "Even when justified a leader must remain dignified."

Trying to correct an unprofessional situation when you are truly innocent is a real test of whether one has the ability to *Intern CEO Style*. Within 48-hours of this embarrassing incident, I emailed this professor about what had transpired. Once again, I reiterated my interest in the position and apologized for acting unprofessional in his office. I don't recall his exact response, but I do know I felt much better afterward; though I was still under the assumption that my participation in the internship had been rescinded. I even called the FBI and told them that I was no longer eligible for the program, but the hiring representative indicated that she didn't see a problem with me interning with them.

Still, I prayed to God for what was surely a miracle. Within a couple of weeks, I received a call from an FBI official telling me to come in to meet my supervisor, and set a work schedule. I couldn't believe it! To this day, I don't know if my professor contacted the FBI or not, but in retrospect, I believe I handled the situation like a maverick and it paid off.

My Internship with the Federal Bureau of Investigation (FBI)

The basic structure of this internship was:

Shadowing	Part-time—Spring semester
Unpaid	Solo intern
Local	No paid tuition
Instructor supervision	No job offer
Academic credit	

Life as an FBI Intern

After many months of being under intense investigation, the internship *finally* began. Just as I did with my internship on Capitol Hill, I put on my favorite business suit and drove to the FBI building. Previously, when I arrived to this building for my interview and polygraph examination, I had to stand on the outside of the massive brick building (that sits inside of a steel security gate) while waiting to be buzzed in for the gate to open. Once I was inside the gate and then the actual building, I was ordered to go through a metal detector post to be searched. Then I had to wait in the executive reception area for an FBI agent to come get me. This portion of the building had an absolutely elegant design and feel.

It had the appearance of a White House welcoming room where guests would be seated before the President appeared from behind the discreet doors that were strategically embedded inside the nicely glossed wooden walls. I tell you, just by sitting in this polished reception room, I felt as if I was definitely *Interning CEO Style*!

Although I enjoyed the sight and warmth of the reception area, when I reported to work on my first day as an intern I was happy to enter the building through the employee entrance. Now that I was officially an intern, I had access to the entire building with my FBI work ID that had to be swiped before entering various sections of the highly secured building. I was assigned to work with the Violent Offenders Squad—a unit that investigates bank robberies, murders, drug crimes, gang activities, and missing person cases.

Some internships don't lend themselves well to students for hands-on experience, and as a federal law enforcement agency, this was one of them. My involvement in this program was very similar to the shadowing experience I had with the Metroparks Ranger Department.

Even though this was a shadowing experience, I was still able to learn many FBI investigatory tactics and techniques. I assisted agents in searching for missing links to cases by conducting Internet research, reviewing phone records, transcribing audio recordings, and providing my perspective on incidents.

For example, I had the opportunity to review the files of a missing person's case and the strategies that were implemented, in hopes of solving the case. I also sat side by side with agents when they discovered leads to new suspects, and later, stopped by the suspects' homes with them, for questioning.

During another occasion, I was the first person to review tips and leads from a case that was aired on an episode of the *America's Most Wanted* show. This was awesome for me because as a kid, I grew up watching almost every episode of *America's Most Wanted* every Saturday night. And many years later, as a college student and FBI intern, I was able to watch this show provide coverage on a case that I was directly involved with on a day-to-day basis. The case was broadcast on Saturday, and when I reported to the FBI office on Monday, the agents gave me an unopened envelope that was comprised of the tips and leads—this was really *too good to be true*!

I also watched this particular case air on local news segments during the time I interned with them. Watching these media broadcasts helped me to understand how important these types of cases are to the general public.

Interestingly, I was personally familiar with someone who was under investigation in a different case. In particular, a major crime was committed against one of my family members, and the FBI was searching for the suspect. My family member asked if I could disclose any new information on the case, and the supervisory agent allowed me to offer fresh facts and updates. I felt good about being able to do this because it made my relative feel a little better to know that the case was still being actively pursued after being open for so many years.

In another case, I was part of a drug raid that was literally a couple of houses down from the residence of one my friends. As the FBI agents searched the house, I was responsible for watching the girlfriend of the suspect, after he had been taken into custody. This was a good experience for me, as I was able to work behind the scenes of a drug raid and interact with a suspect's companion. Given the circumstances, the girlfriend thought I was an agent, and I often found her asking questions of me about whether or not she was headed to jail too. She said she thought she was dreaming when she awakened to her door being kicked-in during the middle of the night and her home flooded with FBI agents who were pointing loaded guns— what a "real world," law enforcement experience.

Outside of this live action, I enjoyed watching and editing the tapes in which agents would use private informants with a hidden audio wire and camera attached to them, to make a drug transaction. On nearly every occasion the drug dealer's first phrase was, "You ain't no cop are you?" There were countless times when the informant had to convince the other party that he was an honest customer who had no association with the police. Every time I heard this question I laughed so much because the informants did a good job with their acting.

On a more serious note, I became so emotionally attached to one case that I used it as motivation to help me condition for a FBI special agent fitness test, which some new applicants had to pass before being hired as an FBI agent. I actually participated in this test with four new applicants and passed it with a pretty good score!

Internships can help boost your confidence, as when I attended a couple of elementary schools with the agents, and the students referred to me as a special agent. I loved every moment of the recognition! In fact, because many people know that one needs to be a top quality student and citizen to participate in an internship with the FBI, my family, community, and peers, granted me tremendous respect by often referring to me as an actual FBI agent, as well.

Friends asked me to look up others who owed them money, so they could find them. I even had someone tell me that they had lost their phone and wanted to know if I could somehow obtain all of their saved numbers from a computer owned by the FBI. I told them to stop watching so much CSI on television because things didn't quite work like that in the FBI in real life! Lol.

Receiving Academic Credit

This unpaid internship required a 20-hour work week, in addition to school, but the rewards for me were huge. I was able to find a college instructor who was willing to oversee my internship experience, so I could receive academic credit. I made sure to meet with her once every two weeks to discuss my experiences. A simple required journal and an essay that highlighted what I did on a weekly basis, helped me gain college credit for my internship experience—receiving academic credit was a good trade-off for wages.

Letting Your Light Shine

When I surveyed some students for this book, one asked what they could offer to an internship organization. I was surprised by this question because most students go into an internship or even an actual job, wondering what the employer can offer them. However, this particular question that the student asked indicated to me that he had figured it out. He knew that an internship is a relationship that's usually comprised of three parties: a student, the school, and the actual internship organization. Consequently, all of these parties should be able to bring something unique to the table.

We already know that an internship is supposed to give you good, "real world" experience if nothing else, while the school offers academic credit and/or guidance. But these should be in exchange for the student's creativity, energy, hard work ethic, quality productivity, and commitment to the school and internship organization.

To me, this simply means that you must let your light shine as you represent your school, organization, family, and community. You must make it a point to be a positive role model by always maintaining an image that's as solid as gold. If nothing else, this is what you can offer an organization. Of course, you can be a superstar if you provide a substantial, innovative element to your organization. However, you can also become a superstar by simply maintaining a positive attitude and avoiding gossip and/or any situation that compromises your integrity.

After reading this chapter, you may have noted that I didn't make any major breakthroughs on the cases or other tasks that were assigned to me. But I did consciously display a positive and respectable character at all times. I was fortunate that people noticed this and recognized my efforts with respect, as I had let my light shine by *Interning CEO Style.*

Intern CEO Style
Leadership Principles

> **Visit your Career Services Department for internship guidance.** Speak with your Career Services Department or the appropriate internship representatives before looking for an internship. By doing this you will learn all of the rules and regulations of the internship process. This is an important step because you don't want someone later saying that you didn't follow the school's internship guidelines and as a result, are not eligible for academic credit, or to even participate in the internship program. Taking this action may also help you retain the school's faculty members as valuable allies.

> **Apply to internships well in advance.** Plan on applying to internships at least four to five months in advance of the application deadlines. So if you want to acquire an internship for the Fall semester that begins in September, you should start the application process at the beginning of May or June. Some internship application processes are so extensive (such as the FBI) to where you may have to begin applying and collecting the necessary information and documents up to one year in advance.

> **Maintain a high G.P.A.** Try your best to maintain a cumulative grade point average of at least a 3.0. Many of the better internships will require this; however, if your G.P.A. falls short, don't be afraid to still apply if you truly believe you have what it takes to get the position.

> **Be a maverick and maintain a good reputation.** Always consider yourself as a superstar and positive role model for your peers, school, internship organization, and community. Let your light shine so others can be influenced by your positive demeanor and achievements.

> **Never S.E.T.T.L.E. for Something Else That Takes Little Effort.** If there's a challenging internship position

or other goal you have in mind, go for it! You tenacity and perseverance will pay off sooner than you expect.

➢ **Always be the bigger person, and don't burn any bridges.** "Even when justified always remain dignified." This simply means even when you are not in the wrong, as an intern, many times you must swallow your pride and be positive. It's also important for you to never act on your anger or frustration—doing such a thing could create a disaster and negatively impact your future opportunities.

➢ **Keep a clean background history.** Don't engage in anything that may later appear in a background check and cause you to become disqualified from an internship position. This includes experimenting with drugs, creating a bad credit report for yourself, and/or racking up traffic violations. Let's face it, you may make a mistake in one of these areas at some point because no one is perfect; but you do want to minimize these types of incidents, as much as possible.

➢ **Secure all private information.** Never disclose any private or confidential information about your organization to family members or friends. Usually upon hiring, your supervisor will share with you the types of information that can or cannot be shared with individuals outside of the organization. When in doubt, you should ask your supervisor for those guidelines.

How I Got My
Master's Degree
for Free

5

"The best things in life are free."

American Proverb

"Anyone who understands his *why* can endure almost any *how.*"
Friedrich Nietzsche

The Application and Interviewing Process: I was Determined to go to Graduate School for Free by Doing Whatever it Took!

When you begin an internship you're often uncertain as to why you are there and what you want to absorb from your experience. Sometimes it might feel like it's something you're doing only because it's what your parents and teachers have encouraged you to do. However, there's a reason for internships, outside of the concern of pacifying these influential people.

While *Interning CEO Style*, you must take your internship journey just as seriously as you do a career. If you stay dedicated to your internship career, it's certain that many benefits will come to you, and much faster than your peers. Dedication to your internship career could ultimately lead you to nicely paid internship opportunities, a free graduate degree, and eventually, your dream job. Although many internships are unpaid, I encourage you to still pursue them while keeping in mind that these experiences will ultimately lead to paid internships and more.

Up to this point you learned how I earned money and respect from my internship experiences. In this important chapter you will discover how I earned my master's degree absolutely free of charge—and you can too! My only financial responsibilities were books and a bi-annual parking permit for my car. Enrolling into graduate school for free became a goal of mine after I began to notice I was racking up a lot of loans, while in undergraduate school. One day I said to myself that if in the future I could ever go to college for free, I was going to do it—no questions asked—by whatever ethical method it would take.

To this end, after graduating from undergraduate school I decided to enroll into graduate school, with the hopes of obtaining a graduate assistantship. A graduate assistantship is a form of an internship that typically allows students to teach a course or become a research assistant to a professor. In all honesty, I was a little skeptical when applying for graduate assistantships because I thought the free education component was too good to be true. In view of the substantial loans I had to obtain for my bachelor's degree, I just didn't believe that a person could actually go to school and not pay one red cent for tuition.

Cynically, I applied to Kent State University, The University of Akron, and Cleveland State University by completing the appropriate applications to be considered for a graduate assistantship. Kent responded first via letter indicating they didn't have a position available for me. I didn't let this discourage me because this is the exact reason why I applied to more than one school for a graduate assistantship; and you should do the same when applying for internship positions. I didn't want to rely only on one school, as I understood the importance of expanding my options.

Within a week of receiving the Kent notice, Akron called and wanted me to interview for a graduate assistantship. I subsequently interviewed with them, and was offered the position on the spot. But I didn't take the offer right then. Instead, I asked if I could take a few days to consider their offer. Actually, I was stalling for a couple of days in hopes that Cleveland State would also come through with an offer. Cleveland State was my school of choice because it was closest to my residence and had a very reputable graduate program in public administration.

Well thank God—right before my deadline to make a decision for Akron, my first choice school called and indicated they had a position for me. Cleveland State offered me a secretarial position in one of the school's offices. I thought this was the best position for me to accept since it was going to pay for my graduate degree at my preferred school.

It came time for me to contact Akron and Cleveland State to inform them of my decision as to whether or not I would accept their respective offers. So what did I do? I remembered that the Bible says, "A wise man has many counselors." So I once again called two of my most active mentors, Steve and Linda, and scheduled a meeting with them to discuss my options. These are the very same mentors who helped me make the decision to pursue an internship on Capitol Hill, so I had much confidence in their guidance. Can you believe that they encouraged me not to pursue *either* offer?

I thought they were crazy and implying I shouldn't enroll into graduate school at all. However, to my surprise, they did support my master's degree goal more than I could ever imagine—they put a deal on the table that I had never received in my entire academic life. Here was the deal—all I had to do was concentrate on my studies and apply for other graduate assistantships in my downtime—and they would pay full-tuition for my first semester of graduate school!

This act of kindness encouraged me beyond degree. They were willing to put thousands of dollars into my success. This is when I vowed—again—that, "I would never ever let anyone believe in me more than I believe in myself." Even though I wasn't sure if I had the talent to successfully complete graduate school, they believed in me and were willing to show me by putting their money where their belief was. After the semester had started, it only took two weeks for this *CEO Style Intern* to procure a graduate assistantship, which ultimately ended up paying for my two-year graduate school education.

My Internship as a Graduate Assistant with Cleveland State University Maxine Goodman Levin College of Urban Affairs' Center for Health Equity

The basic structure of this internship was:

Hands-on	Part-time—Fall and Spring semesters (two consecutive years)
Paid	Solo intern
Local	Graduate college tuition paid
No instructor supervision	No job offer

My Days as a Graduate Assistant

Working as a health research assistant was a very different experience for me, since my background was mostly criminal justice at this time. But you know the one experience that qualified me for this position? The unpaid internship with Congresswoman Stephanie Tubbs Jones' office. Although I had no real experience with health issues since taking a health education class in high school, the interviewer thought I was a good match for this graduate assistantship almost completely based on my Capitol Hill experience.

Although I wasn't very familiar with the field of health, I thought it wouldn't be a difficult area to work in since it dealt with equity and disparities. This was the driving factor for me because I learned all about social disparities, in general, while interning with Congresswoman Stephanie Tubbs Jones. Actually, I didn't even know the definition of 'disparity' until she used the term when describing her motivational passions, and explained the word to me. Shortly afterward, I discovered that rectifying disparities was one of my passions, as well.

So I was a health disparities researcher, and blessed because my tuition was fully paid *and* I received a biweekly stipend, for the two years it took to earn my master's degree in public administration. This was a very good experience because it introduced me to another form of justice that was outside of the criminal justice system. I met and worked with some of the top health experts and professionals in the

Greater Cleveland region, along with passionate community residents.

Can you believe that I only worked 10-hours a week for all of these wonderful benefits?! Once again, this is what it's all about. *This* is why you should develop an internship career by securing all the internships you can, starting in high school; because it will later make you an attractive candidate for sweet positions like this one.

The Center for Health Equity was awarded a grant from the National Institutes of Health to research obesity and its effects. In particular, we conducted Community-Based Participatory Research (CBPR) that deeply involved lay citizens. This CBPR project's goal was simply to involve community residents in the research as much as possible while endeavoring to reduce obesity.

This community approach allowed us to hear the concerns of residents and let them shape a program of their choice by using their knowledge of the community. The traditional research approach is the opposite of CBPR because researchers develop programs without much input from community residents in this conventional framework.

We fulfilled the participation goal of CBPR by conducting many surveys, interviews, focus groups, and meetings with community residents and public officials. In addition to performing the aforementioned tasks, I researched best practices that consisted of other obesity related programs being conducted throughout the country.

Although I found this to be boring at times, it was fairly significant because we used this list as an example for ideas to show residents how their respective program could be structured. As you probably know, there are many ongoing health projects in the nation, so I had to determine which ones were most relevant to our objectives; this was an extremely crucial step in the research process.

The importance of this assignment was found in the notion that the information I provided would assist in triggering thoughts that would be used to build a local public health program. I compiled the best presentation that I possibly could. Make certain that you do the same with your work assignments. Use your creativity and proficient computer skills to make some dynamic and colorful reports, Power-Points, and other similar presentations—this extra effort will make you look like a rising star!

The CEO Style Intern as a Community Servant

Performing community-based activities throughout this internship was life changing because it provided the experience I needed to found my own community 501 (C) (3) nonprofit organization. The name of the organization is Community Healers Acknowledging Needs Goals and Expectations (C.H.A.N.G.E. Volunteers, Inc.). Over the years, C.H.A.N.G.E. Volunteers, Inc. has grown tremendously as our members continue to diligently serve the community by volunteering time and services to underserved populations at nursing homes and shelters.

We also empower ourselves by engaging in self-empowerment programs and activities that emphasize the development of leadership skills. We are comprised of teenagers and adults who just have a desire to make the world a better place. I'm extremely grateful that my internship experience helped me cultivate the necessary skills to successfully lead C.H.A.N.G.E. Volunteers, Inc.

Success is in Right in Your Pocket

As a result of my graduate assistantship and volunteer experiences, I was recognized as a leader among graduate assistants and interns at Cleveland State University. College administrators asked me to speak at the annual concluding internship luncheon. My assignment was to give a talk about my internship experiences and how I achieved success to current interns and their supervisors.

This was perfect for me because I enjoy letting my light shine through my motivational speaking endeavors. I like encouraging other students to understand that success is right in their pocket! And the same statement applies to you, success is right in your pocket, as well! But you have to stretch and reach deep down inside and pull it out. Once you realize this you will be able to do whatever you put your mind to.

You should understand that you may have to work at some internships in which you may not have much interest, in order to achieve your success. However, to summarize a famous quote by Nietzsche, if you understand the *why* (or the big picture), you should be able to endure almost any *how* in attaining and/or maintaining your internship!

I didn't always enjoy the mundane assignments I completed during my graduate assistantship experience, but I understood that my *how* was through this internship. And my *why* was for me to earn a free graduate degree—take time now to evaluate the *how* and *why* for your goals.

Things will not always be easy as you navigate your internship career, but you must learn how to succeed in spite of tough times. Someone once told me that sometimes you will have to laugh when things aren't funny and agree when you disagree, in order to achieve your goals. But if you do decide to disagree as an intern, be careful because inexperienced interns sometimes don't know how to disagree appropriately with others in a professional manner.

I once interned with someone who always challenged and disagreed with the employees at our organization. This intern wasn't accepted too kindly and many people gave them a hard time because the intern was too outspoken at times. Sometimes this person's disagreements were legitimate, but the delivery was confrontational.

Being less aggressive and outspoken doesn't mean that you should be "phony," but it's all about growing and understanding the culture of your organization. As you progress through your internship, though, you will likely have learned how to disagree professionally with your colleagues during appropriate situations. To this end, one of your goals should be to learn how to communicate effectively. This can be achieved by watching how others interact at your internship. Excellent communication skills and awareness of the organizational culture are essential for successful interns!

Intern CEO Style
Leadership Principles

➢ **Apply to numerous internships.** Don't limit yourself by applying to only one internship at a time. Apply to multiple organizations so you can increase the probability of an offer from at least one of them.

➢ **Ask for time to make an internship acceptance decision, if it's needed.** If you are offered a position and not sure if you're ready to accept it, kindly and wisely ask if you can take a few days to consider their internship offer.

➢ **Seek guidance and mentors.** Seek those who have been in your shoes before, and use their advice. In particular, during your internship career, utilize your resources, such as high school or college administrators, family, and friends—you will be able to turn to them during difficult times. They should be able to offer sound advice that will help you succeed and prevent you from making silly, but costly career mistakes.

➢ **Pick the best internship.** If you are offered two internship positions simultaneously, thoroughly analyze the pros and cons of both positions and talk to people you trust for their opinions. Select the one that is most beneficial for your career goals.

➢ **Be resilient and tenacious.** Understand your *why* so you can endure any *how*. Your *why* is for experience, money, and the success an internship can inspire. Since internships are relatively short, you should be able to tolerate any *how* (within reason). This means that you should be able to execute the boring stuff that you may be responsible for completing.

➢ **Tackle the boring stuff.** Even when you are assigned a tedious project, find something meaningful in it and try to conceptualize the bigger picture. Generally speaking, your work will fit into a larger goal of the organization. Sometimes this is a test to see how well you work with smaller, mundane tasks. Just smile and perform them well. When you think the time is appropriate, meet privately with your boss (in a professional manner) to suggest that you have more value to offer, and ask for more substantive work.

➢ **Master your communication and presentation skills.** Communication is very important in any organization. Watch others to witness the interactive culture, so you can learn how to communicate and give presentations effectively. Or ask your supervisor for some tips to help you communicate successfully within the organization. It's also important to speak professionally by using proper English at all times. Also, use your creativity to make dynamic reports and presentations—organizations will appreciate and recognize the extra spice that you add!

My Dream as an
Intern that Finally
Came True

"If one advances confidently in the direction of his dreams, and endeavors to live the life, which he has imagined, he will meet with a success unexpected in common hours."

Henry David Thoreau

The Million-Dollar Email I Received from a Friend

One day as I was checking my email, I noticed that a friend of mine had forwarded me an email. Since the subject line was "NASA Internship," I almost didn't open the message because I thought she had emailed the wrong person. I didn't major in science or engineering, so I wondered why she would send an internship link for an internship with the NASA to me.

Out of curiosity, I opened the message and noticed that it was for a summer internship with NASA OIG. I scrolled down to determine what the acronym OIG stood for; I learned that OIG means Office of the Inspector General. Never in my life had I heard of an "Inspector General," but the description on the internship announcement offered brief details about their primary duties as investigators.

NASA's Office of the Inspector General—Office of Investigations primary responsibilities includes investigating governmental fraud, waste, abuse and some agency administrative issues. A sampling of administrative issues encompasses employee sexual harassment and severe employee government credit card abuse.

Once I learned that the pay for this internship was $15 an hour and understood that their primary mission was to investigate federal white-collar government crimes, I thought to myself, this might be a great opportunity for me to gain more criminal justice experience!

I was already working as a graduate assistant with Cleveland State University's Center for Health Equity (CHE), but I thought the internship with NASA's OIG would keep me busy in the upcoming summer, since I had summers off from CHE. As a result, within the next week or so of opening the NASA OIG link, I decided to officially apply. It was difficult for me to meet the application deadline because I was already working as a graduate assistant *and* in graduate school full-time.

However, as usual, I typed my application and quickly notified the people who I hoped would write letters of recommendations for me. In addition, I wrote the required one-page essay that explained why I wanted to intern with the OIG. I poured my heart and soul into that essay since the application indicated there wasn't going to be an official interview. This meant that the essay was my biggest chance to directly communicate why the OIG should select me as their summer intern.

Once I finally completed the application, I mailed the materials in an official U.S. Postal envelope, for a professional appearance. Furthermore, while at the post office, I selected the postal option that required a signed delivery receipt.

After a few anxious months without hearing anything, I finally received a package in the mail from NASA. It contained a letter that stated I had been selected for the position. I immediately thanked God for blessing me once again! It was such a surprise because I acquired this position without even having a personal interview with NASA.

After my excitement settled, I emailed my new supervisor to schedule a time for me to stop by the office so I could meet the staff before the official start date of my internship.

You will understand more specifically why this was a million-dollar email when you read the next section.

My Internship with the National Aeronautics and Space Administration (NASA) Glenn Research Center's (GRC) Office of the Inspector General (OIG)—Office of Investigations

The basic structure of this internship was:

Hands-on	**Full-time—Summer**
Paid	**Multiple interns**
Local	**No paid tuition**
No instructor supervision	**No job offer**
No academic credit	

An Intern's Dream come True

I was very excited on the day I began my internship because I was back in my passionate field of criminal justice. When I reported to the agency, the special agents and support staff welcomed me to the organization for the summer with kind regards.

My supervisor, Karl, spent a lot of time during the first week sharing knowledge with me through our daily talks. He showed interest in learning about my ambitions for law enforcement so he could determine how he might help me achieve my goals. He even purchased a book for me that defined the many different federal law enforcement career opportunities. For the first couple of weeks I was tasked with the assignment to read through this resourceful book and other background information on NASA's OIG.

I can honestly say that all of this reading in the summer wasn't too exciting, but I understood the importance of it because it helped me understand the organization's values and principles. Learning the values of an organization is vital, as this information can be used to assess where and how you will best fit within the agency.

There was another summer OIG intern, Diego, who attended school at the University of Southern California. And since I'm an Ohio State Buckeye's fan, he and I talked a lot of trash to one another about football. The two of us came from different backgrounds and environments, but we had a great working relationship. Having someone else to brainstorm and attend social functions with definitely made this internship experience more enjoyable for both of us.

Our task for the summer was to investigate an administrative case that the special agents didn't really have time to fully pursue. One day the agents came into our shared office space and dropped many years of files, that were stored away in dusty boxes, on the floor. I can recall thinking to myself that this will be a very daunting task. Nonetheless, I was excited to give it a shot. The agents jokingly told us we could have the summer off if we were able to crack the case. After hearing this, we diligently worked on this case in hopes of trying to demonstrate our positive work ethic.

Of course I can't go into all the details of the case, but I will share with you as much as I'm allowed to in this book. The case was very unique because it dealt with an individual who mailed sexually harassing and threatening letters to NASA GRC's employees—he often signed the letters as "The NASA Spanker."

You've seen this kind of case on the evening news—reports that someone anonymously sent hate mail or threatening letters to the offices of public officials. But instead of public officials, this particular individual targeted some of his colleagues. In 1996 he began issuing letters to women through GRC's interoffice mailing system[13], and to their homes via the U.S. Postal mail service. He drafted concise, one-page letters that always included a particular story line, which indicated the type of fantasized relations he desired to have with the targeted females.

Approximately ninety-five percent of the letter was false and the other five percent would be true. For instance, he might say, "I noticed you walking to your car with a blue sweater on at 2:00 pm on Wednesday, and I loved the way you walked." This part would be true, but the remaining portion of the letter was comprised of only exotic, fantasy based thoughts.

So Diego and I began to review the documents to get a feel for what was going on. We requested any necessary or additional supportive information through the agents because they had access to several different public and commercial databases that allowed us to investigate this case from a few different angles. The special agents had worked on this case periodically through the years, so there were many reports and different analyses to read and build on.

---

[13] This is an internal mailing system within GRC that allows employees to mail their fellow coworkers documents and packages.

Initially, the two of us read through many of the letters to try to understand what we were up against. During this process I read a letter or two that was written and mailed directly to the OIG, stating that they would never ever catch him. These letters were like fuel for my soul. As you may have realized by now, I'm very competitive, so I took this as a direct personal challenge.

After we heavily familiarized ourselves with the case by reading over most of the documents, it was time to actually determine how to tackle this case. The agents had many suspects in mind and listed their reasons as to why they were on a target list. So I often referred to this list and as I started to analyze the case, one suspect in particular began to look very good to me. I shared this inkling with my buddy Diego, but he decided to take a different approach in investigating the case.

He chose to analyze the actual stories within the letters while I took a look at the facts of the case. For example, the suspect only mailed a handful of letters to his victims' residences, and mostly utilized NASA's internal interoffice mailing system. I was especially interested in the dates of those letters he sent through the U.S. Postal mail system, and the cities from which the letters were mailed.[14]

I also inspected the envelopes for return addresses, which I felt were another key element. The addresses were not of his actual residence, of course, but I noticed he used the same vicinity as that of his family members and friends' residences to make a fictitious return address. My theory was that he would visit someone and use a random address number from down the street, as a return address.[15]

Also, even though most of his handwriting on these envelopes was intentionally disguised, I was able to review some of the suspect's original, non-disguised handwriting samples. We collaborated with the security office at another NASA center to receive writing samples from a sign-in sheet that documented his name when he traveled there for work. While reviewing this evidence, certain letters and characteristics of his writing style started to catch my eyes. Consequently, I began to have a deeper interest in this guy.

---

[14] I was able to get this information because the post office stamps each mailed letter with a date and the city from which letters are mailed from.

[15] The special agents were able to provide me with the addresses of his relatives by searching a commercial law enforcement database.

As I discovered new bits of evidence that led me to believe that this was our guy, Karl and the other agents became more interested in what I had to say. They again began to examine several other aspects of the case. It didn't take long before Karl decided he would become more directly involved by taking Diego and I on surveillance watches of this person of interest.

Although as time progressed our team was able to discover many incidental reasons as to why we thought this guy was responsible for the letters, we still had to uncover a concrete piece of evidence in order to obtain a judge-issued search warrant for his residence and office. This process was sort of slow, in my opinion, pointless. I felt we had gathered enough data to justify linking him to the offense. However, all of this circumstantial evidence we spent lots of time collecting wasn't quite strong enough. We yet needed to find a smoking gun. In an effort to search for this, one of the agents came up with the grand idea of conducting a trash-run on his property.

A trash-run is simply when a law enforcement official discretely collects a person's trash *after* it's laid on the curb, which makes it public property. (You've likely seen this tactic of evidence-gathering in numerous law enforcement TV shows or movies.) It took nearly a whole month to score. The first few times we were unsuccessful; the initial attempt failed because the suspect didn't put any trash out that week. On the second attempt, we just missed picking it up—the trash truck beat us to it. And on the third try, he was outside watching. It wasn't until the fourth time that Diego was able to quickly grab the trash and jump back in the car.

When we arrived back at the office we carefully and methodically picked through his garbage. We had to be extremely cautious in handling the trash to make certain we didn't destroy any evidence. There wasn't much to work with, but guess what? As we neared the bottom of the bag, there were fragments of letters similar to those in the case files.

As much as I had known he was our guy, I was still amazed and couldn't believe it! Diego and I were extremely shocked and excited. *My dream had finally come true.* I played a significant role in cracking a ten-year-old case. This is why I refer to the internship announcement message as *the million-dollar email*—having this opportunity to help solve a case with a federal law enforcement agency made me feel like I had just won a million dollars!

Now that we had found our smoking gun, we were able to draft requests and proposals for the judge to issue the two search warrants. Also, we created a plan that outlined how the search warrants would be executed. It took maybe three or four weeks to complete this necessary procedural process. (A little longer than the five minutes it takes policemen on TV to obtain a warrant.) In addition, we contacted several local law enforcement agencies for their support in conducting the search and seizure process.

Finally, our plan was set. We received the search warrants from the judge and confirmation from the other agencies that they would support our request.

The day came for us to execute all of our detailed and carefully crafted plans. It was still pitch black outside when we all met in the parking lot at about 5:00 a.m. There were approximately fifteen law enforcement officials (plus me) altogether, and we discussed our specific roles over coffee and doughnuts. (Yes, law enforcement personnel love their doughnuts.)

My recollection of this day is still quite vivid. We arrived at the suspect's residence and everyone took his or her positions[16]. Before I knew it, I heard an agent give several knocks on the door yelling, "Police with a search warrant. Open the door!" The agent repeated the required law enforcement command two more times, and shortly after, was ordered to take the door off. He began pounding away with a door rammer until it finally broke through.

The suspect, who was close by the door, was taken down to the ground and handcuffed. I couldn't help myself—during this time I began to quietly sing the "Bad Boys" theme song of TV's *Cops* show—"*Bad boys, bad boys, whatcha gonna do, whatcha gonna do when they come for you ...*" This was definitely a law enforcement intern's dream that had come true at an unexpected hour, as the quote at the beginning of this chapter indicates.

We thoroughly searched the house and found record books of his harassing letters. And with much satisfaction, I had the opportunity to assist in the interrogation process of the suspect. There were two other agents and I, who took turns drilling him with questions. During this process he was sweating profusely, as if he had just finished playing in the Super Bowl.

---

[16] I observed from a distance, until the scene was safe.

After the interrogation process we actually spoke with some of the FBI agents I used to intern with, to consider some collaboration opportunities on the case. This was a good experience for me because I was able to gain a better, first-hand understanding of how federal law enforcement agencies work together to investigate cases.

Diego didn't have the opportunity to participate in the collaborative efforts with the FBI nor the evidence collecting process. He returned to California for school, prior to these investigatory activities being conducted. Fortunately, my internship lasted just long enough for me to participate fully in the whole investigatory process!

I would like to acknowledge that the special agents always kept us out of harm's way and were very receptive to many of our ideas. More specifically, this is the closest I have ever worked with any of my supervisors on a day-to-day basis. With Karl, I would often forget that he was the boss. He didn't hide in his office or act as if he was too busy to mentor his interns.

After my internship ended, he actually tried to convince his boss that the OIG's hiring standards should be lowered so I could apply for a vacant agent position. When I say "lower the standards," I mean to allow recent college graduates the opportunity to compete for the special agent position, rather than requiring an applicant to have a college degree, *plus* many years of federal law enforcement experience, in order to apply. Although his boss did not modify the standards, I was very honored and pleased that Karl advocated for this *CEO Style Intern* to be considered for such a prestigious federal agent position, though I was so relatively young.

Trouble is Sometimes Inevitable and Unavoidable

Although I did a good job in this internship, I still managed to stir up a little trouble during this experience. However, it was something that anyone might have had a problem with ... one day on my arrival to work, I mistakenly ran into an employee entrance steel guardrail that lifts to allow entry to the parking lot.

Here's how it happened. After swiping my badge for entrance, I pulled up to the guardrail and when I tried to stop and wait for it to lift, my vehicle's brakes went out—geesh. The car wasn't moving forward fast enough to break through the rail; so instead, it kept rolling until my windshield became stuck *underneath* the steel rail.

The only way I could get out of this jam was to put the car into reverse gear. Of course, I couldn't stop in reverse, either, because I had no brakes! (Are you laughing yet—hilarious right?) I ended up in a grassy area and quickly shifted the car into the park gear and came to a stop. Get this—the parking lot's security camera captured every second of the incident! Lol.

I'm sure the agents still watch this video footage when they need to get a good laugh for the day. I honestly think it might be able to make it on an episode of *America's Funniest Home Videos*, if they were to submit this terribly embarrassing, yet funny incident.

This is another example of why you want to do everything in your power to demonstrate a good image and character while *Interning CEO Style*. You just never know when something will happen that's unexpected and threatens your carefully crafted image. As you will read in the very next chapter, possessing a spotless reputation gives you a margin for error that can save you from being considered as anything less than a stellar intern.

Intern CEO Style
Leadership Principles

➤ **Investigate all internship recommendations.** When someone supplies information to you about an internship, check out whether or not you think you will be interested. It just may be a disguised opportunity that will make one of your dreams come true.

➤ **Get recommendation letters.** For the people you wish to write recommendation letters on your behalf, ask them for their assistance well in advance of your internship application deadline so they will have ample time to submit it for you. Give them all the necessary information they need so they won't be bogged down by having to dig for it. Also, if applicable, offer to provide a SASE (self-addressed, stamped enveloped) for the mailing of your letter. You want them to have to do as little work as possible to complete your request.

➤ **Mail your application documents from the post office.** When you have to mail an application, take it to the post office and use a 9 in. x 12 in. envelope to package your materials. Also, use the postage option that requires the receiving party to sign for the package—doing this conveys that you are about business!

➤ **Give it your all.** As Henry David Thoreau says, "If one advances confidently in the direction of his dreams, and endeavors to live the life, which he has imagined, he will meet with a success unexpected in common hours." Pour your heart and soul into whatever project or task you must complete, no matter how daunting or impossible it may seem to accomplish. You will be surprised what you can achieve during your internship with your fresh and creative perspective.

➤ **Be a humble team player.** If you do play a significant role in creating or accomplishing something, never take full credit for it. Many projects and assignments that you participate in will be part of a team effort, so make certain you acknowledge it as such.

➢ **Inquire about a full-time position.** If you are interested in acquiring a job with your internship organization after you graduate, ask your supervisor for information on any open positions and the application process. By doing this you will be expressing to the organization that you have a genuine interest in becoming a full-time employee.

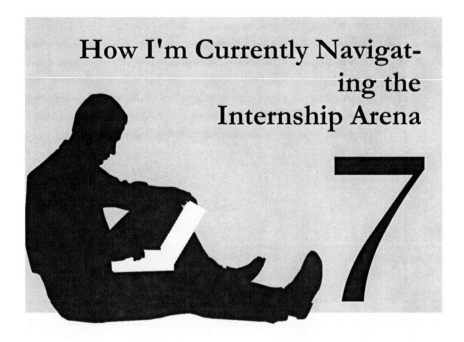

How I'm Currently Navigating the Internship Arena

"I always wanted to be somebody, but I should have been more specific."

Lily Tomlin

"It is only when we have the courage to face things exactly as they are, without any self-deception or illusion that a light will develop out of events, by which the path to success may be recognized."

I Ching

The Application and Interviewing Process that I Took for Granted

While at my previous internship with NASA Glenn's Office of the Inspector General (OIG)—Office of Investigations, I kept my eyes open for future opportunities. Though aware that there likely would not be any other criminal justice related internships available at NASA, I thought there might be other areas in which I could use my public administration education.

One day, I received some information on NASA's Cooperative Education (Co-op) program. I reviewed the program description and was surprised that it offered so many perks to an intern. Among some of the benefits were great pay (the highest I've ever earned), sick and vacation days, health benefits, professional development training, paid holidays, and most importantly, a job offer upon a successful graduation from college.

Of course there were many opportunities for students who had interests in science, math, engineering, and technology. However, there were some professional business administrative opportunities available, as well. This appeared to be a terrific opportunity that I couldn't pass up.

I expressed my interest in the Co-op program to my OIG supervisor, Karl, and he scheduled a meeting with the program's coordinator. During our meeting, Karl expressed interest in me completing my Co-op experience with the OIG, if I were accepted into the program. However, due to some structural organization issues, the OIG couldn't be appointed a student to Co-op with their office at that time. The coordinator explained that there were other positions to which I could apply, nonetheless.

I was all for it and asked her to explain the process to me. She indicated that there was an upcoming Co-op fair within the next couple of weeks and encouraged me to attend. Since it was scheduled during work hours, I had to ask Karl for permission to attend the event. He approved of my attendance, and on the day of the fair I made certain to have plenty resumés in hand. I learned that representatives from the many NASA organizations would have booths set up to conduct on the spot interviews, so resumés were essential.

I attended it with little preparation because I wanted to see how effective my skills were in spontaneous interviewing situations. Typically, I would have taken several days to prepare; but I just felt like winging this event, as a personal test.

Now keep in mind, by this time I had completed many internships and generally knew what company interviewers looked for and expected from an intern. However, I don't recommend that you act this boldly if you are new at the game. Honestly, if I had known the actual value of this Co-op program, my preparation process would have been like none other—I would have worked extra hard to prepare for the internship fair.

While at the fair, I semi-interviewed with two representatives from the Logistics and Technical Information Division (LTID). They seemed to be interested in my background and achievements, but thought I might be a better fit in a different division. As a result of divulging my education and internship experiences to the representatives, I believe they forwarded my name to the Procurement and Security Divisions; but I ended up leaving the job fair uncertain as to whether or not I would be accepted into the Co-op program, since I wasn't offered a position on the spot.

Within the following week, I received a call from the Procurement Division requesting I come in for an interview. Of course I agreed and immediately began to research this organization's mission and objectives. As with most of my other internship experiences, I had no clue what the heck procurement was, but I also wasn't afraid to learn all about it.

On the day of the interview I was reminded of my interview with the Metroparks Ranger Department. There were four managers sitting at the table when the secretary escorted me into the room. Instead of being intimidated this time, I was completely ready for this surprising challenge.

Once the interview started they fired away with their questions, and I fired back with my responses. As we talked I made certain to make eye contact with them all. My favorite part of the interview came when I had the opportunity to ask them questions. I was eager because it allowed me to have a little break from talking so much, and apply some of the lessons I recently learned from the book *How to Win Friends and Influence People* by Dale Carnegie. Referring to people by their names is one principle from this great book I applied in particular during the interview.

Since there were four interviewers, this was a perfect time for me to try my name memory trick. So I inconspicuously sketched a diagram of where the interviewers were sitting and placed their names in my sketch accordingly. Every so often I discretely glanced at my sheet in order to register their names. The big test would come at the conclusion of the interview when we would all shake hands in parting.

The moment arrived—I shook their hands and confidently referred to each of them by name. Guess what? It worked! It was like I had just performed an astonishing magic trick. They all recognized my accomplishment and jokingly asked how I was able to do something that was so impressive.

Considering how well the interview had proceeded, I left with the impression that I was accepted into the Co-op program and would begin my first assignment with the Procurement Division. I was excited and patted myself on the back for a job well done. During the following week, however, I received a letter in the mail indicating that my first tour would be with LTID. But, I didn't have any problems with this assignment—I was just excited to be in NASA's Co-op program.

The goal of this program is for students to gain practical work experience while working in different divisions within NASA to give them broad experience, and find the best fit by their graduation date. After graduating, students are typically offered full-time positions on a non-competitive basis. This simply means that students are offered a job without having to re-apply and undergo the interview and application process all over again.

This is a pretty sweet deal, and in my opinion, Co-op programs are one of the better internship experiences because they often provide full-time job opportunities to students, upon a successful graduation from college. Actually, after I completed my master's degree I was offered a full-time position, but decided to decline it because I wanted to pursue a Ph.D. in public administration with research interests in emerging leaders and leadership.

Speaking of which, not only did I attain my mater's degree for free, I'm now shortly about to receive a free doctorate degree, as well. Since I'm completing an internship and have been very successful, Cleveland State University granted me with a tuition grant for me to continue in my education—just another perk for *Interning CEO Style!*

A Stumbling Block, but How I Allowed the World to Conspire for Me

My Co-op assignment was supposed to begin a month later than the usual start date for an intern to begin the Co-op program. It was scheduled this way because Karl wanted me to help wrap-up the case I played a huge role in solving with his office. The special agents were in the process of reviewing the evidence that was seized from the mail harassment suspect's home in hopes of taking the case to trial.

So when I was accepted into the Co-op program, Karl requested that I stay an extra month before I officially started in the new program.

His request was granted and since I was soon to be an official Co-op, I reported to the security office to undergo the process of obtaining a new work identification badge. This badging process is where I ran into my stumbling block.

All I had to do was complete some paperwork and have my photo and fingerprints taken. Simple, right? This process that took all of about 20 minutes nearly ruined my entire career at NASA. Foolishly, I made a statement and a very innocent gesture while taking my photo. Since the badging official was friendly, I thought I could interact with them in a laid back fashion.

My actions weren't meant to be anything outlandish or derogatory; however, when instructed to pose for a picture, I jokingly made an immature hand gesture that suggested I was affiliated with a gang. I made certain to remove my hands from the picture, though, before the actual snap of the picture. It was a totally innocent motion made in fun, and I thought the badging officer understood the humor of it. However, I guess it was construed to be offensive and as a result, the incident was officially reported management.

The next day I arrived to work had unexpectantly asked me what happened during the badging process. Karl explained that the he received a phone call in regards to my unprofessional incident. As a result, their office was pushing for me to be fired, and therefore terminated from the Co-op program. Talk about being blown away by a statement—I was shocked! It was quite weird coming from a case I helped solve, and now the shoe was on the other foot and *I* was being investigated.

I spoke with an OIG agent and he encouraged me to apologize to the badging officer for my actions. Although I didn't feel as if I intentionally did anything wrong, I swallowed my pride and personally apologized for my very immature behavior. I professed that I would never demonstrate any unprofessional behaviors or tendencies of any kind in the future.

This was definitely a lesson learned because I now make a conscious effort to be professional in the workplace at all times. However, I let my guard down that time because I thought I did something funny that turned out to be offensive. So my innocent joke actually backfired on me in a tremendous way!

During your pursuit to *Intern CEO Style,* never joke, do, or say anything that can be taken out of context. Such remarks could come back later to haunt you—think twice, and always be professional.

Fortunately, some officials were willing to go to bat for me and give me another chance. Now if I had been anything other than a good intern, I would never have made it through this process. More likely than not, I would have been fired; however, my supervisor and a few other employees spoke on behalf of my character and work ethic. They knew I would never intentionally attempt to offend anyone, so they came to my aid and hoped I would learn from my mistake.

This is why I recommend that you perform your best at all times, so you can catch a break when the inevitable happens. Sometimes life shows up at your doorstep and there's nothing you can do to prevent unfortunate circumstances from transpiring. But if you always or even often under-perform and display a negative character, you will not have much room for a break when the inevitable unexpectedly pops up.

If you are honest and work hard, the world will eventually conspire for you and give you a *get out of jail free card,* as you chase your dreams. And you have to *chase* them because sometimes they appear as if they are running away from you, but you must actively pursue them until they come true. Like Charles Luckman once stated, "Success is the old ABCs: Abilities, Breaks, and Courage." This badging incident was definitely a *break* for me since I received a second chance because I had the *courage* to apologize and the *ability* to be an excellent intern—thank God for second chances!

My Internship (Cooperation Education Program) with NASA Glenn Research Center's (GRC) Logistics and Technical Information Division (LTID)

The basic structure of this internship is:

Hands-on	**Part-time—Year round**
Paid	**Solo intern**
Local	**Graduate college tuition paid**
No instructor supervision	**Job offer**
No academic credit	

Developing Executive Policy as a Co-op

Since I was under a semi-investigation as a result of the badging incident, I couldn't assist in finalizing the case with the OIG. This would have been a conflict of interest because the OIG had to review personal statements and investigate the complaint. Consequently, I simply began to work where I had initially been assigned for the Co-op program, which was with LTID. I was disappointed, but understood that I had to move on and not let that incident steal my joy.

Upon reporting to LTID, I really didn't know what I was getting myself into. However, a maverick is ambitious, courageous, and understands the importance of taking advantage of all great opportunities. The first opportunity I had was to assist several employees with some of their work responsibilities. This work pertained to monitoring and evaluating logistics operations contracts.

For example, the transportation, janitorial, waste management, publishing, and metrology services are all offered by LTID. Many of my colleagues and I are Logistics Management Specialists; and as civil servants, we enforce federal policies and monitor services that are carried out by contractors.

By my third or fourth month with LTID, an employee retired and this was a very good opportunity for me to fill a void within the organization. As a result of this staff loss, I was offered the responsibility of his duties. I agreed to accept the position that pertained to managing a portion of GRC's transportation contract.

Although I don't have any direct experience in contract management, fleet management, or energy conservation, my master's degree in public administration paired with my fearlessness to try anything new, have equipped me with some fundamental skills that empower me to effectively implement and develop federally mandated transportation policies and programs that I will talk about in the subsequent paragraphs.

My primary responsibilities center on transportation services and fleet management. Contractors perform mechanical duties on government motor vehicles at our onsite auto repair shop, and I serve as the government representative over this part of the contract. I monitor their work performance, budget, and other work related activities to ensure their operation's effectiveness and efficiency, while adhering to federal regulations.

NASA also established some environmental policies that must be achieved through recycling and waste management initiatives.

Some of my other responsibilities include charting and presenting these benchmarks and metrics to employees and management at NASA.

Perhaps my most exciting and rewarding areas of responsibilities are GRC's alternative fuel program and initiatives. President Barack Obama signed an executive order for federal agencies to reduce their impact on global warming and foreign oil dependence epidemics. Consequently, several others and I are responsible for implementing this presidential mandate that was established in an effort to decrease gasoline, and increase alternative fuel (Ethanol, Compressed Natural Gas, Biodiesel, etc.) consumption for GRC. I feel deeply rewarded when I watch President Obama render his primetime speeches and boldly assert that America will support renewable energy practices, starting with the federal government. I always feel as if he's speaking directly to me because I develop such projects and programs on a daily basis—it is such a phenomenal experience to actually be able to implement policies that come straight from the President of the United States.

Another title I wear is the Fare Subsidy program administrator for GRC. This program was established by a presidential executive order some years ago to decrease federal employees' motor vehicle and fuel impacts on the environment. To achieve this, a policy was developed that indicates civil servants can receive free bus and transit cards for their commutes to and from work, if they meet some minimal eligibility requirements. As the administrator, I make certain the program is run effectively and resolve any problems posed by the members.

Community Outreach and Social Networking Activities

I'm very active, too, in many community outreach programs and activities at GRC. I decided to become a member of NASA's Speakers Bureau so I could have opportunities to speak at colleges, schools, and other community events. I look forward to informing students and the public about career opportunities and updates on what's going on at NASA. I have also attended career fairs/days and served as the keynote speaker for a couple of school ceremonies. In addition, I actively tutor students each year through the Cleveland Federal Executive Board's Tutoring program—giving back to your community is very important and I encourage you to get involved in outreach and social networking activities if you have the opportunity to do so.

To expand my social networking circle, I participated in a Martin Luther King Essay contest held at the GRC and was shocked by the attention I received. A committee selected winners for first, second, and third places, and I received the first place honor. I had no clue as to how much positive recognition I soon would be obtaining for writing the best essay in this contest.

I was highlighted in the monthly newsletter, received many requests for a copy of my essay, and fielded multiple congratulatory phone calls and emails—I felt like a miniature movie star!

Due to activities like this, I am now well-known throughout GRC, and it's rewarding that many people refer to me as a future a future Center Director of GRC. There are over 3,000 employees there, yet every so often I run into people who say, "Oh, *you're* Antoine. I have heard so much about you and I'm happy to finally meet you."

This is what it's all about—producing quality work, networking, and getting involved so people will recognize you as a leader, rather than just a nameless "intern." Actively participating in these types of networking opportunities increases your visibility within the organization and conveys that you aren't just an ordinary intern—it shows that you are *Interning CEO Style*!

An Intern with an Intern

During this internship experience with GRC my supervisor allowed me to mentor and supervise a summer intern, Derric Studamire, who is a student at Morehouse College. Oftentimes people have rhetorically asked me how I, as an *intern*, was able to have an *intern*. My typical response is that I just work as hard as I can and enjoy developing others.

I also make it a point to mentor a handful of summer interns who aren't under my official supervision, in hopes of helping them optimize their experiences at GRC. This is very important and rewarding because I enjoy motivating students to pursue their dreams by encouraging them to utilize their natural, God-given abilities and learned skills.

Tailor Making My Internship Just for Me

OK, now pay close attention because this is a huge take away section for not only this chapter, but *Learn to Intern CEO Style*. One of NASA's primary missions is to explore objects and ideas. Keeping this in mind, it took me almost nine years of internship experiences to realize that internships are all about exploration, as well. If you really want to distinguish yourself from your peers during your internship exploration pursuit, you must set high goals and standards that can be reasonably attained. Just as the astronauts, engineers, and researchers of NASA literally reach for the moon, you too should reach for the moon during your internship experiences.

As a result of my extensive internship career, I've learned how to get the most out of boring experiences. Actually, this is the first time I have been able to take a conscious and deliberate initiative to tailor an internship experience just for me. In the past, I thought I had to follow and navigate an internship exactly the way it was set up by the organization. However, I now know that most internship supervisors are very supportive of an intern's visions, goals, and ambitions.

My interests, for instance, are in leadership within public organizations. Consequently, I shared this with my current supervisor and she now allows me to meet with and shadow members of NASA's senior management team. Many of these high-level officials are aware of my ambitions and have offered very informative career advice and information because I made certain to personally meet with them. In addition, I recently had the opportunity to take an independent study leadership course with GRC's previous director, Dr. Julian Earls. These intimate interactions with NASA's leadership have helped me develop even more confidence that will assist me in becoming an executive leader in the future.

I also have had the opportunity to take advantage of professional development and training courses that are offered through my agency. These premier training sessions are conducive to the growth of individuals within NASA. I'm not required to participate in some of this training, but it's obviously in my best interest to be involved with as many of them as possible.

As part of a formal mentoring program, I've been given the opportunity to be mentored by two well-respected NASA officials—Dr. Dexter Johnson and Mrs. Lori Manthey. We meet formally and informally during lunch and other social outings to build a healthy professional relationship. This mentoring program is invaluable because I'm able to receive good information and guidance about strategies that assist me not only in becoming a better intern, but an overall person, as well.

This is how you are supposed to make things work for you in your internship by participating in activities that will enhance your professional development. Your experience should not be the same as any other intern's because your dreams, goals, and ambitions are different. Just as Lily Tomlin's quote at the beginning of this chapter states, you should be very *specific* about what you want to be or gain from your internship experience.

So think about what your interests are or what you would like to experience by the end of your internship tenure. Once you've done this, personally craft and shape your internship so you will have the opportunity to benefit as much as you can from your experience. Write down the goals you want to achieve and meet with your supervisor to learn whether or not they can be accomplished—I refer to this as MapQuesting your internship.

If you are a passive intern who only performs the job description of the internship, you will miss out on many of the internship's valuable opportunities. But by the same token you want to make certain you have a handle on your work assignments before you engage in any extra developmental activities. Sit down with your supervisor or mentor and develop a plan (see my plan template in Appendix J). With their assistance, many aspirations you desire to achieve should be attainable if the plan is reasonable and properly aligned with the goals of the organization.

The key to this is prioritizing your responsibilities and objectives. You do not want to be viewed as an intern who participates in many social or training activities, but never produces any quality work, in a timely fashion. If you develop a personal plan and know how to prioritize your daily projects and responsibilities, your experiences should be just as awesome as mine!

Intern CEO Style
Leadership Principles

> ➤ **Refer to interviewers by their names during your interviews.** Identifying interviewers by name gives a more personal touch and helps build positive rapport while you are being interviewed.

> ➤ **Navigate your internship.** If you intern for a large agency, don't be afraid to navigate the infrastructure and later apply for different internships within that agency. Or if it's possible, ask if you may spend a day or so with a different office within that organization, to become more familiar with other areas. Use this opportunity to soak up as much exposure to as many career options as possible.

> ➤ **Find a mentor within your organization or agency.** Start with your supervisor and ask for suggestions of the best way to proceed in finding a mentor. More likely than not, they will be impressed by your ambition and pro-activeness and want to help you, or even serve as your mentor.

> ➤ **Take notes during your interview and ask questions.** Take a notebook and pen to write quick notes while you are interviewing. Make certain you take short-hand notes and don't zone out while taking them. The act of note taking conveys that you are seriously interested in what's being discussed. Also, asking intelligent questions demonstrates your genuine interest in the position—you definitely want to do this.

> ➤ **MapQuest your internship experience with an Internship Plan.** Meet with your supervisor so you can develop an Internship Plan that's tailor-made just for you. Your internship experience should not be exactly the same as other interns in that organization because you have different dreams, goals, and ambitions.

➢ **Maintain a high-level of professionalism.** Never ever let your hair down in an unprofessional manner around those you are unfamiliar with. This could come back to haunt you later.

➢ **Practice good office etiquette, especially with phone and technology communication.** In this technology age, it's common for students to communicate in a short-hand format, such as the correspondence that takes place via Instant Messenger and text messaging. But, that type of communication is not appropriate in the workplace. Make certain that you take note of the following advice.

> ➢ **Emails.** All emails and any other types of documentation should be drafted in a professional format that follows the standard rules of English. You should also ask your supervisor to provide you with some examples of the office's communication style.
>
> Do not forward any funny or other types of chain emails through the office that could be considered unprofessional or offensive to anyone. Keep all communication strictly professional.
>
> ➢ **Cell phone.** Though it's tempting to install musical ringtones on your phone and identify your known callers by them, when you are an intern, it's in poor taste for your phone to ring loudly with music. By the same token, if you are searching for or completing an internship and receive calls from your job, your ringback tone should be a standard ring—not a song.
>
> Also, I recommend that your voicemail greeting be professional. Again, this means no music playing in the background or jokes aimed at your friends.
>
> These are important points to remember because you just don't know what types of music or jokes might offend someone who's calling to offer you a job! Or, you don't want to come off as unprofessional to your current internship supervisor, who may decide to call you for something.

Only speak on your cell phone during your official work breaks, and be mindful of your conversation if you're talking while in an office or professional setting.

Text messaging friends or listening to music via iPod in meetings and other formal settings is considered rude. Be mindful of how you operate your fancy technology gadgets because you don't want them to be the demise of your internship.

➢ **Office phone.** Your office phone should always be answered professionally by using the greeting that you were instructed to greet callers with during your work shift. Lastly, your family members and friends shouldn't call you at work unless it's an emergency.

➢ **Work area and desk.** Keep a clean and organized work area. Your desk and workspace should always remain neat and organized. This is especially important for when you leave to go home at the conclusion of your work shift. Sloppy appearances diminish your credibility and level of professionalism.

➢ **Work hard at all times, so the world can conspire for you when you make a mistake or need a break.** After all, according to Charles Luckman, "Success is a mix of the old ABCs—Abilities, Breaks, and Courage." So always work hard and produce quality work so you can get a break when one is needed.

➢ **Consistently develop your skills through your internship.** Take advantage of as many training and professional development opportunities as possible. Doing this will allow you to effectively develop your skills in a professional environment. But remember to prioritize these by discussing these opportunities with your supervisor.

➢ **Prioritize your daily projects and responsibilities.** Make sure you have a handle on these things before you participate in any social or training activities. Poorly managing your assigned tasks could be the cause of your supervisor not approving of your participation in other professional development opportunities—so make sure you manage them well.

➤ **Review internship blogs.** If you want to discuss current internship topics/discussions or simply review them, go online and find some internship blogs. These forums often provide good advice and relevant information that you can put to use. Check with your supervisor to see if you are allowed to look at these while at work. If you are prohibited from doing so, just wait until you get back to your dorm room to log on from your personal computer.

CONCLUSION

Developing Leaders for Today and Tomorrow

"The only thing to do with good advice is pass it on. It is never any use to oneself."

Oscar Wilde

"Many receive advice, only the wise profit from it."

Publilius Syrus

Passing Knowledge on to You

In addition to implementing transportation policies at NASA Glenn Research Center with the Logistics and Technical Information Division, I was recently assigned to a year long detail with the Human Capital Training and Development Branch to develop a leadership program for current and emerging leaders[17]. This program will be utilized to enhance the leadership skills of rocket scientists, expert engineers, and talented business professionals that are employed by NASA. Although you may not work for NASA, you

---

[17] I work 20-hours a week implementing transportation policies and an additional 20-hours developing the leadership program.

shouldn't feel left out because you can use this book as a developmental tool while you strive to cultivate professional skills and knowledge.

I have been an intern practically my entire academic life and have made a very healthy living from it. Now I'm passing on the internship knowledge I've acquired to students such as you, in hopes of helping you optimize your internship career. Oscar Wilde once said, "The only thing to do with good advice is pass it on. It is never any use to oneself." And I agree with this sentiment!

I'm not completely helpful to our society when I harbor knowledge that I know can help my peers. This is why I decided to provide you with informative and helpful strategies in Learn to Intern CEO Style. Throughout this book I have offered a great deal of advice on how you can succeed in your internship experiences. By sharing my experiences and insights with you in the past chapters, I hope you've learned some of the intricate dos and don'ts of internships. However, all of this information and advice is useless if you do not apply it to your academic and career ambitions. Keep in mind what Publilius Syrus expressed, "Many receive advice, only the wise profit from it."

To this end, in our competitive national economy and job market, you should be eager to accept tips from successful people who have already been where you are trying to go. These tips will help you avoid many stumbling blocks and bad experiences, as you endeavor to cultivate skills that will give you an advantage over your peers.

Internships provide you with the opportunity to meet professionals and see how they put their expertise to work, while you sharpen your business savvy and skills. Some internships are easier than others to find and obtain. But if you are serious about your career and professional development, I encourage you to do whatever it takes to procure as many internships as you can. And once you attain one, be sure to perform at an advanced level by *Interning CEO Style*. Remember, this framework has four essential pillars: you must: 1) Always maintain your integrity, 2) Take personal responsibility over your internship career by customizing your experiences, 3) Develop yourself as a business, 4) Sharpen your soft-social skills and become a "people person," and 5) Consistently produce quality work. Developing and applying all of these concepts will not transpire over night. However, all you have to do is work hard and keep giving it an honest effort and I guarantee you that you will be a standout student and intern, as you strive to explore your dreams.

It is important for you to know that interns are very vital to organizations. If your current internship tasks have you primarily responsible for brewing coffee and providing secretarial responsibilities, meet with your supervisor and express your desire to expand your duties. But in the meantime, you should cheerfully brew the best coffee and be the best secretary—and do it with a smile! Actually, these mundane work duties are often used as tests to determine if the you are capable of enduring the simple challenges. Once this level of work is conquered, you may receive more meaningful assignments.

As I conclude this chapter, I asked some of my internship supervisors to share some brief advice with you in regards to how you could be an excellent intern. Below are the essential insights they wanted to share with you. After reading these remarks, you will find a complete list of the *Intern CEO Style* Leadership Principles.

Advice for You from the Experts

"Interns can have a successful internship experience by using it as an opportunity to learn as much as possible. They can do this by observing what others are doing around them, being good listeners with their supervisors and asking questions along the way. Asking questions about how or why something works or operates is a good thing. Getting a full view and concept of what is happening at the work place. Also asking, when your small assignment is done, if there is something more that you could do."

Clarence Fluker
Former Student Instructor
American Civil Liberties Union of Ohio

"While interning, remember to maintain professionalism in all that you do. That professionalism should direct you to always be excellent at whatever tasks you are performing."

Nichole Griffin
Former Student Instructor
American Civil Liberties Union of Ohio

"Whether it is a paid or unpaid internship, students must do a good job. They must be punctual and able to effectively complete their assignments. They should go the extra mile in terms of making sure whatever they do is done to the best of their ability. They also must be flexible and able to work well with others.

An intern's clothes, shoes, hair, beard, etc. should be neat, and they should dress in appropriate attire for that specific internship. NO nose rings or other extravagant piercings. If at all possible, they should cover tattoos, as well. They must be mindful that internships are not social events, so they should act and speak like they are at work.

Therefore, interns should not share personal stories or information that can leave negative impressions. They should show an interest in the company or organization by trying to learn about functions of the company other than what they are assigned.

Practicing these suggestions will leave a good impression on supervisors as well as other members of their organization. This will allow the organization to give the intern a good reference, as they will be able to positively speak on their work ethic and skill set. This could even potentially lead to a full-time position."

Lillie Blair
Retired Lieutenant
Cleveland Metroparks Ranger—Law Enforcement Department

"Exceptional interns possess several qualities: Attention to detail; dedication to mastering a variety of issues; and a willingness to seek out other intelligent people for answers, ideas, and friendship. These are also the skills that make individuals successful in any profession. However, when starting a professional track record your peers and supervisors may question things about you, but the aforementioned things should not be on that list."

Anthony Quinn
Former Congressional Aide
Office of Congresswoman Stephanie Tubbs Jones

"Interns should try their best to get involved. The smartest way to do that is to observe carefully, in order to learn the "routine" and culture of the organization. Typically, each employee has ways of doing things and making sure that work assignments are completed effectively. The trick is to find or create a piece of that routine that you can take over and make your own. It allows you to become a part of the "flow" of the operation, and makes your presence valuable to the organization. That way, you are most likely to be included. By doing these things you can be sure that you will learn a lot, and make the positive impression that you want to make."

Doug Williams
Special Agent
Federal Bureau of Investigation

"Students need to enter an internship with open minds to new experiences and knowledge. Concurrently, they need to understand that within any internship, they are part of a project team or office staff. Thus, they too can and should bring new knowledge and ideas to the table to move a project forward. This give-and-take experience will enrich both the student and the employer, and make the internship experience beneficial for all parties involved. An internship should be about learning new skills, but also contributing in a meaningful way to the work environment."

Kendra Daniel
Project Coordinator
Center for Health Equity
Maxine Goodman Levin College of Urban Affairs
Cleveland State University

"Students should excel in their internships if they have a good work ethic, perseverance, a positive attitude, social skills, and ability in their respective career field. They also need to find a mentor who will try to provide them with the opportunity to develop and demonstrate their talents."

Karl Strohbehn
Supervisory Special Agent
Office of Inspector General—Office of Investigations
NASA Glenn Research Center

"An intern needs to be open to learning about the organization and position /role that he or she could fill. This means an intern needs to be somewhat flexible and adaptable to uncertainties. An intern also has to demonstrate a strong desire to make a contribution to the organization. This quality will generate a number of positive actions that will act as a catalyst to connect the intern to the work of the organization. In addition, the intern should be proactive in bringing their background and experiences to the organization and willing to communicate and share these experiences for the benefit of the organization."

Mary Lester
Division Chief
Logistics and Technical Information Division
NASA Glenn Research Center

Intern CEO Style
Leadership Principles that Should Always be Applied

1. **Never S.E.T.T.L.E. for Something Else That Takes Little Effort.** If there's a challenging internship position or other goal you have in mind, go for it! You tenacity and perseverance will pay off sooner than you expect.

2. **Let go of your pride.** Never let pride stop you from accomplishing or pursuing your goals. You must be humble and willing to sacrifice some things, in order to advance your career.

3. **Learn from your failures.** Whether it be applying to internships or performing during them, learn from your unsuccessful attempts. If you are rejected or get knocked down, get back up and try again a different way.

4. **Broaden your career horizons.** When putting Mark Twain's quote in the context of internships you should, "Sail away from your safe harbor and explore, dream, and discover" your career path by taking advantage of internships.

5. **Relocate if you can.** Take advantage of an internship that requires you to relocate to a different city, state, or country. With this adventure, you will become familiar with another area and observe a wider variety of people and organizations, outside of your comfort zone.

6. **Know that networking is vital to your success.** Someone once said, "It's not always who you know. But, it's also about who knows you, too." Network to attain your first internship. Network for your next internship. And then ultimately network to attract job offers. Use internship colleagues and supervisors as re-

sources to prepare for your next internship experience or job.

7. **Maintain a high G.P.A.** Try your best to maintain a cumulative grade point average of a 3.0. Many of the better internships will require this; however, if your G.P.A. falls short, don't be afraid to still apply if you truly believe you have what it takes to get the position.

8. **Be a maverick and maintain a good reputation.** Always consider yourself as a superstar and positive role model for your peers, school, internship organization, and community. Let your light shine so others can be influenced by your positive demeanor and achievements.

9. **Keep a clean background history.** Don't engage in anything that may later appear in a background check and cause you to become disqualified from an internship position. This includes experimenting with drugs, creating a bad credit report for yourself, and/or racking up traffic violations. Let's face it, you may make a mistake in one of these areas at some point because no one is perfect; but you do want to minimize these types of incidents, as much as possible.

10. **Seek guidance and mentors.** Seek those who have been in your shoes before, and use their advice. In particular, during your internship career, utilize your resources, such as high school or college administrators, family, and friends—you will be able to turn to them during difficult times. They should be able to offer sound advice that will help you succeed and prevent you from making silly, but costly career mistakes.

11. **Be confident and believe in yourself.** "Never let anyone believe in you more than you believe in yourself," during your internship journey. If someone tells you that you can do something, believe them. If they support their belief in you by going out of their way for you in one fashion or another, accept their confidence in you and don't feel as if you aren't smart or skilled enough. Like the Nike logo says, "Just do it"! Be careful not to be arrogant though while displaying your confidence—all you have to do is produce quality work

while maintaining your integrity, and other people will eventually brag about your talent and skills.

12. **Intern CEO (Creator of Excellent Opportunities) Style.** There are five primary pillars to *Interning CEO Style*, you must: 1) Develop yourself as a business, 2) Take personal responsibility over your internship career by customizing your experiences, 3) Consistently produce quality work, 4) Sharpen your soft-social skills and become a "people person," and 5) Always maintain your integrity. Be mindful that this requires time, as well as personal sacrifices and investments.

13. **Discover your self-concept.** Learn who you are, which values are important to you, and last but not least, your strengths and weaknesses. Work continually to improve them both to develop your character.

Intern CEO Style
Leadership Principles that Should be Applied Before Your Internship

14. **Develop your brand.** Immediately formulate and then convey to people your competitive advantage—work hard continuously to sharpen this brand.

15. **Be proactive, and utilize your resources while pursuing internship opportunities.** Take personal responsibility and ask your resources for help. Don't sit back and wait for someone to get you excited and hyped-up to complete an internship. Notify your resources (family members, friends, librarians, school administrators, etc.) and express your interest to them about acquiring an internship. They may be able to direct you to some excellent internship opportunities. Also, don't forget to use social networking sites like

LinkedIn or Facebook for internship announcements or information.

16. **Visit your Career Services Department for internship guidance.** Speak with your Career Services Department or the appropriate internship representatives before looking for an internship. By doing this you will learn all of the rules and regulations of the internship process. This is an important step because you don't want someone later saying that you didn't follow the school's internship guidelines and as a result, are not eligible for academic credit, or to even participate in the internship program. Taking this action may also help you retain the school's faculty members as valuable allies.

17. **Investigate all internship recommendations.** When someone supplies information to you about an internship, check out whether or not you think you will be interested. It just may be a disguised opportunity that will make one of your dreams come true.

18. **Apply to internships well in advance.** Plan on applying to internships at least three to four months in advance of the application deadlines. So if you want to acquire an internship for the Fall semester in September, you should begin the application process at the beginning of June. Some internship application processes are so extensive (such as the FBI) to where you may have to begin applying and collecting the necessary information and documents up to one year in advance.

19. **Apply to numerous internships.** Don't limit yourself by applying to only one internship at a time. Apply to multiple organizations so you can increase the probability of an offer from at least one of them.

20. **Pursue unpaid internships.** Unpaid internships are still valuable even though you're not receiving monetary compensation, as they often lead to future paid internships and full-time jobs.

21. **Type your applications and forms.** Where possible, type or use other helpful computer software to complete all of the application forms and documents. This gives your application a professional presentation and

demonstrates that you are serious about acquiring the position.

22. **Mail your application documents from the post office.** When you have to mail an application, take it to the post office and use a 9 x 12 in. envelope to package your materials. Also, use the postage option that requires the receiving party to sign for the package—doing this conveys that you are about business!

23. **Prepare for your interview.** Just because you are young and inexperienced, don't be afraid of an intimidating "real world" interview setting. A lot of preparation can help you overcome this anxiety.

24. **Get recommendation letters.** For the people you wish to write recommendation letters on your behalf, ask them well in advance of your internship application deadline so they will have ample time to submit it for you. Give them all the necessary information they need so they won't be bogged down by having to dig for it. Also, if applicable, offer to provide a SASE (self-addressed, stamped enveloped) for the mailing of your letter. You want them to have to do as little work as possible to complete your request.

25. **Thoroughly research the organization you are applying to.** Review the organization's history, goals, and mission statement before the interview. Talk about these aspects and how your skills align with them during the interview meeting.

26. **Know where you're going for your interview.** Some time prior to the interview, ride or walk by the building in which your interview will be held, so you will know exactly where you are going and how long it will take for you to get there.

27. **Pick the best internship.** If you are offered two internship positions simultaneously, thoroughly analyze the pros and cons of both positions and talk to people you trust for their opinions. Select the one that is most beneficial for your career goals.

28. **Refer to interviewers by their names during your interviews.** Identifying interviewers by name gives a

more personal touch and helps build positive rapport while you are being interviewed.

29. **Take notes during your interview and ask questions.** Take a notebook and pen to write quick notes while you are interviewing. Make certain you take shorthand notes and don't zone out while taking them. The act of note taking conveys that you are seriously interested in what's being discussed. Also, asking intelligent questions demonstrates your genuine interest in the position—you definitely want to do this.

30. **Ask for time to make an internship acceptance decision, if it's needed.** If you are offered a position and not sure if you're ready to accept it, kindly and wisely ask if you can take a few days to consider their internship offer.

31. **Thank everyone.** Contact every person who helped you attain an internship position and thank them for their wonderful support.

Intern CEO Style Leadership Principles that Should be Applied During Your Internship

32. **Dress professionally.** To *Intern CEO Style*, you must dress and present yourself like a CEO. Dress to impress at your internship, but don't go overboard. Observe what others are wearing and ask your supervisor for advice about the most appropriate attire. Also, many jobs allow its employees to dress casually on Fridays. Monitor your coworkers' dress style on these days to determine what type of attire is appropriate for Fridays.

33. **Punctuality is a must—be on time.** Being late or tardy is completely unacceptable, so be on time. Better yet, make it a point to arrive between five and fifteen

minutes early to work, meetings, and all other appointments.

34. **Don't abuse a flexible work schedule.** Some internship organizations are flexible to the point where they allow interns to create their own work days and hours. With this flexibility, students may be able to change their work days and hours throughout their internship. If you have a flexible schedule, don't abuse or continuously change it. For example, if you set up your schedule for Monday, Wednesday, and Friday from 9:00 a.m. to 5:00 p.m., don't change from this schedule often. Your colleagues will be depending on you to be consistent with your work schedule as much as possible. Use your flexibility to change your work schedule when you really need it, and it's up to you to determine what constitutes legitimate reasons for using your flexibility.

35. **Always be honest about things, especially your timesheet and office supplies.** Sometimes you will receive permission from your supervisor to alter your timesheet for the benefit of giving you extra time off to study for an exam, or take care of other personal business. However, never *ever* take it upon yourself to alter or fudge your timesheet by your own choice. Moreover, never steal or borrow anything without asking permission for the items. These are a very dishonest practices and could land you in tons of trouble, or even be grounds for terminating your internship. This reputation could follow you for many years down the road, and therefore your chances of getting future internships or full-time jobs would be negatively impacted.

36. **Chronicle your experiences.** Whether it is required or not, keep a journal and take notes on everything you do. This will help you remember what you've learned as an intern. You should also create a portfolio that includes all of your projects and assignments. Put these documents in a binder so they will be organized because you may want to take this to future interviews, to highlight your past experiences. However, allow your current internship supervisor to review the portfolio to

make certain you didn't include any private or confidential information.

37. **Avoid coworker conflicts.** Don't argue with your colleagues or have an attitude if they don't readily accept you. If there's a problem, see your supervisor privately and immediately to resolve the issue. You can also confide in school representatives or your mentors for additional support, especially if the problem is with your boss. Don't discuss your conflicts with anyone at your internship unless you are convinced that you can trust them. Misplaced trust could make the situation worse if they were to report your concerns to the problematic individuals, without your knowledge.

38. **Never criticize or irritate your fellow coworkers.** In my internship experiences, I noticed that other interns would often challenge coworkers and supervisors. They asked difficult questions in hopes of baffling the person, to make them look stupid. In other instances, the intern would purposely irritate other coworkers and do simple things to upset them.

    Examples of some of the things you shouldn't do are 1) Create attention in front of others to point out a coworker's tardiness, 2) Fail to relay phone messages to others, and 3) Speak sarcastically to coworkers, or not speak to them at all.

39. **Always be the bigger person, and don't burn any bridges.** "Even when justified always remain dignified." This simply means even when you are not in the wrong, as an intern, many times you must swallow your pride and be positive. It's also important for you to never act on your anger or frustration—doing such a thing could create a disaster and negatively impact your future opportunities.

40. **Leave your personal problems at home.** Don't discuss personal affairs at work because others might misperceive your statements and make erroneous judgments about who you are.

41. **Be inquisitive and ask questions.** Talk to the people in your internship organizations and ask intelligent questions. Seek their suggestions, tips, and advice that will prepare you for the "real world." Request their recommendations about how you can have a successful internship and career. Access to such professionals is a great resource for you, so use it. Also, doing this conveys your curiosity and interest in your internship responsibilities and the organization as a whole. It also helps you gain free knowledge.

42. **Don't tell others that you have no desire to work for the organization you're interning with, when you graduate.** If you are not certain this particular place or field of work is of long-term interest to you, simply explain to them that you are exploring the professional arena, and may be open to an opportunity with them should it present itself when you graduate from college.

43. **Be careful with online social networks.** Don't log on social networking sites, such as MySpace, Facebook, Instant Messenger, or Twitter while you are at work. In addition, do not download any type of software on the organization's computers unless you have permission. Don't ask to log on social networking sites or download software packages unless you feel comfortable in doing so, and have a truly convincing reason that explains why you need to have access to these products during internship hours.

    You shouldn't have information or pictures posted on any of these accounts that you wouldn't want your employer to see. For some organizations, they use these social networks to scan and dismiss applicants who post crazy photos or unprofessional content on their personal pages. Also, don't post any derogatory statements about your current internship organization or its employees because you could be fired for such postings.

44. **Absolutely no sleeping while you are at your internship.** No matter how boring your work is or a meeting may be, sleeping on the job is an absolute no-no! It's important for you to always stay awake and be

attentive because sleeping on the job is an easy way for you to diminish your credibility, or even get fired.

45. **Make yourself available to the staff.** Help as much as you can with projects or assignments that may require your assistance. If you don't have a lot of responsibilities, be proactive and ask staff members if they need any extra help.

46. **Build positive relationships by expressing gratitude and appreciation to the staff.** Periodically, demonstrate your appreciation for the staff members taking the time to work with and help develop you. Expressing gratitude conveys that you are thankful and unselfish.

47. **Develop strong soft-social skills and work on becoming a "people person."** These skills will help you enjoy and appreciate working in a diverse workforce. Many people will be older than you and come from extremely different backgrounds, but your interpersonal skills should assist you in learning more about others and effectively working with them. You don't have to necessarily be friends with everyone, but you must know how to respectfully maintain healthy professional relationships.

48. **Master your communication and presentation skills.** Communication is very important in any organization. Watch others to witness the interactive culture, so you can learn how to communicate and give presentations effectively. Or ask your supervisor for some tips to help you communicate successfully within the organization. It's also important to speak professionally by using proper English at all times. Also, use your creativity to make dynamic reports and presentations—organizations will appreciate and recognize the extra spice that you add!

49. **Consistently develop your skills through your internship.** Take advantage of as many training and professional development opportunities possible. Doing this will allow you to effectively develop your skills in a professional environment.

50. **Participate in social activities that happen around the office.** If you notice that every Friday someone

brings in doughnuts, talk to someone and find out if you can participate as a Friday doughnut provider. Or if you notice that every so often someone brings in some type of treat for the office, jump right in and bring a treat a time or two. Also, if you are given the opportunity to sit on the planning committee for a holiday party, do it. Doing these types of things show that you are a team player and enjoy being part of the organization.

51. **Accept social event invitations.** Whether it's on or off the clock, accept invitations to hang out with your boss, or even other full-time employees as much as possible. Do this only if you are comfortable with the setting of the event. You will meet many resourceful people this way; it also offers you the opportunity to hold intimate conversations and build more enduring relationships.

52. **Prioritize your daily projects and responsibilities.** Make sure you have a handle on these things before you participate in any social or training activities. Poorly managing your assigned tasks could be the cause of your supervisor not approving of your participation in other professional development opportunities—so make sure you manage them well.

53. **Learn proper meal etiquette.** This is extremely important to practice when you accept social event invitations. Learn how to properly use your silverware and carry-on an informal professional conversation.

54. **Don't engage or get pulled into office politics.** Avoid gossip, maintain a positive energetic attitude, and don't compromise your integrity. You can ruin your image and reputation by engaging in unhealthy office politics, so don't do it.

55. **Secure all private information.** Never disclose any private or confidential information about your organization to family members or friends. Usually upon hiring, your supervisor will share with you the types of information that can or cannot be shared with individuals outside of the organization. When in doubt, you should ask your supervisor for those guidelines.

56. **Be resilient and tenacious.** Understand your *why* so you can endure any *how*. Your *why* is for experience, money, and the success an internship can inspire. Since internships are relatively short, you should be able to tolerate any *how* (within reason). This means that you should be able to execute the boring stuff that you may be responsible for completing.

57. **Tackle the boring stuff.** Even when you are assigned a tedious project, find something meaningful in it and try to conceptualize the bigger picture. Generally speaking, your work will fit into a larger goal of the organization. Sometimes this is a test to see how well you work with smaller, mundane tasks. Just smile and perform them well. When you think the time is appropriate, meet privately with your boss (in a professional manner) to suggest that you have more value to offer, and ask for more substantive work.

58. **Give it your all.** As Henry David Thoreau says, "If one advances confidently in the direction of his dreams, and endeavors to live the life, which he has imagined, he will meet with a success unexpected in common hours." Pour your heart and soul into whatever project or task you must complete, no matter how daunting or impossible it may seem to accomplish. You will be surprised what you can achieve during your internship with your fresh and creative perspective.

59. **Work hard at all times, so the world can conspire for you when you make a mistake or need a break.** After all, according to Charles Luckman, "Success is a mix of the old ABCs—Abilities, Breaks, and Courage." So always work hard and produce quality work so you can get a break when one is needed.

60. **Be a humble team player.** If you do play a significant role in creating or accomplishing something, never take full credit for it. Many projects and assignments that you participate in will be part of a team effort, so make certain you acknowledge it as such.

61. **Find a mentor within your organization or agency.** Start with your supervisor and ask for suggestions of the best way to proceed in finding a mentor. More likely

than not, they will be impressed by your ambition and pro-activeness and want to help you, or even serve as your mentor.

62. **Don't tolerate sexual harassment.**[18] If you ever feel that you are being sexually harassed or placed in an uncomfortable situation, speak with your mentors, school officials, or family members about this for their guidance. They may recommend that you privately confide in your supervisor for them to resolve this unfortunate issue.

63. **Be smart about dating.** Some organizations strictly prohibit dating on the internship. Others are more lenient and allow dating. However, be smart and careful about this. If you decide to date, I would strongly recommend it being someone close to your age. But my first recommendation is to not date at all, as most of these office romances usually turn out to be a disaster.

64. **Review internship blogs.** If you want to discuss current internship topics/discussions or simply review them, go online and find some internship blogs. These forums often provide good advice and relevant information that you can put to use. Check with your supervisor to see if you are allowed to look at these while at work. If you are prohibited from doing so, just wait until you get back to your dorm room to log on from your personal computer.

65. **MapQuest your internship experience with an Internship Plan.** Meet with your supervisor so you can develop an Internship Plan that's tailor-made just for you. Your internship experience should not be exactly the same as other interns in that organization because you have different dreams, goals, and ambitions.

66. **Navigate your internship.** If you intern for a large agency, don't be afraid to navigate the infrastructure and later apply for different internships within the agency. Or if it's possible, ask if you may spend a day or so with a different office within that organization, to

---

[18] I didn't experience any sexual harassment cases, but I wanted to provide some information on this topic for you.

become more familiar with other areas. Use this opportunity to soak up as much exposure to as many career options as possible.

67. **Maintain a high-level of professionalism.** Never ever let your hair down in an unprofessional manner around those you are unfamiliar with. This could come back to haunt you later.

68. **Practice good office etiquette, especially with phone and technology communication.** In this technology age, it's common for students to communicate in a shorthand format, such as the correspondence that takes place via Instant Messenger and text messaging. But, that type of communication is not appropriate in the workplace. Make certain that you take note of the following advice.

   a. **Emails.** All emails and any other types of documentation should be drafted in a professional format that follows the standard rules of English. You should also ask your supervisor to provide you with some examples of the office's communication style.

   Do not forward any funny or other types of chain emails through the office that could be considered unprofessional or offensive to anyone. Keep all communication strictly professional.

   b. **Cell phone.** Though it's tempting to install musical ringtones on your phone and identify your known callers by them, when you are an intern, it's in poor taste for your phone to ring loudly with music. By the same token, if you are searching for or completing an internship and receive calls from your job, your ringback tone should be a standard ring—not a song.

   Also, I recommend that your voicemail greeting be professional. Again, this means no music playing in the background or jokes aimed at your friends.

   These are important points to remember because you just don't know what types of music or jokes might offend someone who's calling to offer you a job! Or, you don't want to come off as unprofessional to your current internship supervisor, who may decide to call you for something.

Only speak on your cell phone during your official work breaks, and be mindful of your conversation if you're talking while in an office or professional setting.

Text messaging friends or listening to music via iPod in meetings and other formal settings is considered rude. Be mindful of how you operate your fancy technology gadgets because you don't want them to be the demise of your internship.

   c. **Office phone.** Your office phone should always be answered professionally by using the greeting that you were instructed to greet callers with during your work shift. Lastly, your family members and friends shouldn't call you at work unless it's an emergency.

   d. **Work area and desk.** Keep a clean and organized work area. Your desk and workspace should always remain neat and organized. This is especially important for when you leave to go home at the conclusion of your work shift. Sloppy appearances diminish your credibility and level of professionalism.

69. **Never end your internship on a bad note.** Completing your internship in good standing is essential because you never know if you will need help or support from someone within that organization in the future.

70. **Find out if you can intern again.** Some internship organizations allow previous interns to come back for another complete or partial internship experience. An example of a partial experience would be interning with one of your previous organizations during your winter break from school. Interning again is an excellent way to stay in the pipeline and keep your foot in the door.

71. **Inquire about a full-time position.** If you are interested in acquiring a job with your internship organization after you graduate, ask your supervisor for information on any open positions and the application proc-

ess. By doing this you will be expressing to the organization that you have a genuine interest in becoming a full-time employee.

Me as a lawyer during a mock trial at the ACLU

Me with the Metroparks Rangers

My supervisor, Anthony, and I on Capitol Hill.

Congresswoman Stephanie Tubbs Jones and I on Capitol Hill

Me at the FBI

Me working on a case at the FBI

Me facilitating a focus group at the Center for Health Equity.

My Partner In Crime, Diego, and I at NASA Glenn's Office of the Inspector General.

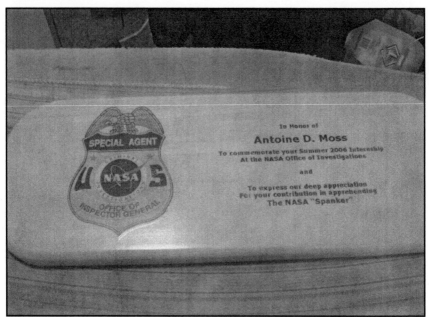

Plaque I received from NASA Glenn's Office of the Inspector General.

My intern, Derric, and I at NASA Glenn's onsite auto repair shop.
Photographer: Michelle M. Murphy, NASA GRC

Me at a NASA Generation Y Leadership Symposium.

PART TWO

Practical Internship
Guidance and Advice

In this section I offer some brief, but useful advice for you on seeking and completing internships. I encourage you to conduct an Internet search for more in depth advice on any of these Appendix topics. Your Internet search will help you discover sample documents (e.g. cover letters) and many other useful internship materials. Internet search engines are powerful resources, and they're free—so use them! You can also take a trip to the library to find books that address these topics more in depth.

How to Find Internship Opportunities

A APPENDIX

The first step in locating an internship is through the utilization of your resources. This recommendation is invaluable. Some of your resources are Career Services representatives, family members, friends, and library representatives. Discuss with them your career aspirations and what your goals are, as they pertain to acquiring an internship. This can be done formally by scheduling a meeting with them or informally by just speaking briefly with them over the phone to ask specific questions.

Scheduling a meeting time with a Career Services representative or a career counselor may be much easier for college students than high school students. The Career Services Department is a gold mine for college students. Oftentimes, these representatives feel as if students fail to take full advantage of the services they offer. However, this should not be the case for you because you are a maverick and desire to gain a competitive advantage in the job market, over your peers.

The Career Services Department should have mostly all of the resources you need. Representatives of this office can help lead you and hold your hand (figuratively speaking) during your internship career. They can assist you with your cover letters, resumé, interviewing skills, informational interviewing, and provide you with many other services.

With your persistence, after one semester of working with Career Services counselors, they should know your name and all about you, without having to check their files. This is an excellent achievement that separates you from being just another ordinary student at your college. Due to their many internship contacts, they should be able to assist you in obtaining internships over and over again so you can have an internship career.

Many colleges have career or internship databases that you must register with in order to receive their internship notifications or announcements. Make it your duty to register and upload your resumé, or whatever information they request. Once again, many students are passive and feel as if it's not important for them to acquire access to this system. However, continuously signing in and updating your profile is essential for your internship success.

High school students may not have an actual Career Services department, so if you are unable to obtain help from a career counselor, I encourage you to speak with one of your teachers to request their help. Your teachers should be willing to assist you due to your proactiveness and their natural passion to see their students excel.

Other forms of resources can be found in your family members and friends. A friend can be someone who is a peer or an individual who's much older than you, such as your mentor. Officially notify them of your interest in acquiring an internship. Share with them your goals and dreams so they will keep their ears and eyes open for prospective internship opportunities that may interest you.

Another resource can be discovered when you visit a public or college library to obtain some guidance from the librarians. They will be able to point you in the right direction by helping you access databases, online searches, and much more.

Take it upon yourself to browse the Internet for internship materials or opportunities—don't forget to use social networking sites like LinkedIn or Facebook for internship announcements or information.

In some instances (when browsing the web), this information may be difficult to locate and won't jump right out at you. However, if you are serious about an internship career, you will work as hard as necessary to uncover even the obscure opportunities.

Once your resources offer you some advice, tips, or leads, make certain you research the additional information. Don't expect your contact to do any extra work for you, unless they offer. For example, don't expect them to obtain and provide detailed information for you on an internship. No. You must be prepared to perform all of the legwork that's necessary to attain an internship. However, oftentimes people do voluntarily offer additional assistance, at which time it's okay if you take them up on their offer.

One popular way to get you more exposure is by conducting informational interviews. You can schedule an informational interview with a person of interest to ask questions about their profession and other career guidance or advice about internships. The interview can be scheduled as a phone or in-person interview. Make certain you ask their interview preference and availability. You should work around their schedule the best you can since they are doing you a favor.

It's important to note that you are just interviewing for information, and not a job. Nonetheless, be professional, on time, and ask intelligent questions that you have already pondered and prepared. This interview should be followed up with a thank-you letter.

Lastly, it's important for you to attend career fairs that are hosted by your school or other local organizations. I recommend you contact all local colleges, libraries, and community centers to learn about future job or career fairs. Sometimes there are restrictions as to who can attend, but many times these events are open to the public.

If some information about an internship is provided to you and you have an interest in it, you should apply for the position. Make certain you carefully read and understand the internship position description so you will know exactly what you are applying for. Some interns don't do this and acquire an internship that turns out to be a bad fit, but you shouldn't make this same mistake.

If accepted, then successfully complete your internship and return to your resources (by this time you may have some new ones) for some more prospective internship information. Follow-up on any leads or tips you receive and apply to more internships.

By the same token, if you are not accepted into an internship program, you should still return to your resources for information. When repeating the process, be sure you don't turn into a pest to your resources. Use your discretion to make certain that you don't go back to people over and over again after they've provided you with the most help and information they reasonably can.

See the Internship Search Conceptual Framework to view a visual depiction of this internship search process. This diagram can be found on the last page of this Appendix.

References and Recommendation Letters
You should develop a list of references before applying for internships. Contact people[19] you think would be comfortable with speaking positively on your behalf. Ask them if you have their permission to list them as a reference contact. You should always keep an updated list of at least three reference professionals with you when applying for internships.

You also want to gather a list of several people who are willing to write an actual recommendation letter for you, as well. This list can be comprised of the same people that are on your reference list. When you approach someone to write a letter on your behalf, you want them to do as little work as possible. This means you must gather all of the necessary background information and materials for them, so all they have to do is write and mail the letter. Give them a written description of the position, along with the name and address of where the letter should be mailed. Offer to provide a SASE (stamped, self-addressed envelope). They may or may not take it, but this shows you are appreciative and considerate of their kindness. Finally, don't over-use or burden your resources. That's why I recommend a list of at least three people, so you can rotate your reference and recommendation letter contacts.

Apply to Multiple Internships
I can't say it enough—apply for multiple internships. These opportunities are competitive, but the more internships you apply to, the more you increase your chances of attaining one. It's also vitally important that you don't wait until the last minute to apply. For example, don't try to find a summer internship the last month before school's out for summer break.

---

[19] It is noteworthy that many times the application specifies that family members can't be used as references.

Most applications for internships have to be submitted four to five months before the actual start of the internship, so you have to carefully plan your activities.

Example timeline: A) Begin internship search on September 1, 2010. B) Identify an internship(s) to apply to. Start completing the application process and gathering all of the required documents and materials documents (e.g. transcripts and recommendation letters) on November 1, 2010. C) Submit your internship application by the deadline date of February 1, 2011. E) Begin internship on the start date of June 1, 2011.[20]

However, I must note that some internship application processes are so extensive to where you may have to begin applying and collecting the necessary information and documents up to a year in advance.

Completing and Mailing Application Materials

If you can, get a Career Services representative or someone else to review your work as you complete the application process. Particularly, your letters, resumés, essays, and personal statements should be reviewed for any errors. Everything should be thoroughly proofread for flow, consistency, and grammatical errors.

All of your materials and documents should be pristine—no grease, food, or any other sort of spot or stain should get on them. The paperwork shouldn't be folded excessively. If you decide to fold things, it should be neatly done. But my recommendation is not to fold the items, if you can help it. You can avoid folding the documents by purchasing a 9 in. x 12 in. envelope from the post office.

When mailing your application packet, select the optional service that requires your recipient to sign for the package. This post office presentation gives your submitted materials more of a business orientation.

You should contact the internship organization by phone or email after five business days, to check on the status of your application. However, if the internship announcement specifically states that you shouldn't contact them to inquire about your application status,

---

[20] Between February and June, there may be other steps you may have to take (e.g. an interview) depending upon how extensive the internship organization's selection process is structured.

don't contact them. You simply have to wait and hope that they contact you first.

Internship Links[21]

Below you will find some links you can access immediately to become familiar with actual internship descriptions and announcements. For a complete listing of private and government internship opportunities across many professions, I recommend browsing through the *Princeton Review's Internship Bible.* This book lists thousands of available internships; and sifting through its many lists may seem intimidating, but all you have to do is review the internship categories you're interested in and go for it!

1) www.careerbuilder.com

2) www.doi.gov/hrm/employ5.html

3) www.experience.com

4) www.groovejob.com

5) www.internjobs.com

6) www.internsource.com

7) www.internweb.com

8) www.makingthedifference.org/federalinternships

9) www.opm.gov/careerintern/QandAof12-20-00.asp

10) www.opm.gov/employ/students/intro.asp

11) www.pmf.opm.gov

12) www.publicservicecareers.org

---

[21] These websites were accessed on October 15, 2009.

13) www.students.gov

14) www.studentjobs.gov

15) www.summerinternships.com

16) www.wetfeet.com

17) www.whitehouse.gov/government/wh-intern.html

18) www.vault.com

Internship Search
Conceptual Framework

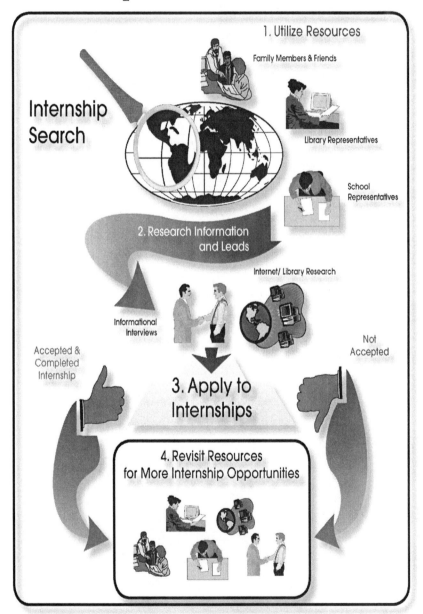

Writing Cover Letters

B
APPENDIX

Cover letters are used as an introduction to your resumé. This document is placed before your resumé, and is used to inform the organization of your interests in a particular position—so it has to be convincing and persuasive, if you want them to go on to read your resumé. It is also an excellent opportunity for you to highlight your specific strengths that relate to the position.

The cover letter should be succinct and polished. As with all of your other written communication, it should be proofread thoroughly to check for flow and grammatical errors.

In the first paragraph, some information that conveys your familiarity with the organization should be stated. The next paragraph should specifically list the position you are applying for. The next section or paragraph should underscore your skills that directly align with the position and organizational required skills. The closing paragraphs should re-indicate your desire to intern with the organization. It should also state that you appreciate their time and will follow-up with them soon.

Make sure you sign your name in black or blue ink right above your typed name to close the letter.

Your cover letter should not be printed on "multi-purpose" copying or printing paper. Visit an office supply store, such as Office Max, and purchase high quality paper with a weight of 24 lb. and at least 25% cotton fiber. No loud or bright colors—I recommend the colors of white or ivory. Do not attach or insert your picture on your cover letter unless the application packet specifically lists it as a requirement for submission. The envelope for your cover letter should be of the same quality and color paper as your letter.

See sample cover letter on the next page.

Sample Cover Letter

Blaza Dean Moss
6 Prime Zone Street
Boston, MA 02101
555-555-7878
bdmoss@circle.com

April 9, 2008

Mr. Sammy Blue
Director of Sports Internships
The For Kids Charity of Boston
17 Lane Circle Square
Boston, MA 02101

Dear Mr. Blue:

The media attention that you have recently received for The For Kids Charity of Boston speaks to the great work that your organization has done within the community. I too, maintain the desire to change the world by instilling hope, courage, and optimism in the next generation of leaders. The Nonprofit Leadership Internship Program's goals and objectives directly align with my career ambitions.

From my life and educational experiences, I have developed:

- great community planning and investment skills,
- a positive rapport with the Boston community through my volunteer service involvement, and
- excellent communication and presentation skills.

My enclosed resumé offers only a snapshot of my skills, talents, and abilities that I have continued to develop as an ambitious student. I would like to personally meet with you to discuss more in depth how, as an intern; I could help The For Kids Charity of Boston advance its mission.

Thank you in advance for taking the time to review this cover letter and my attached resumé. I will follow-up with a phone call to you in the near future, to see if you need any additional information about me while completing your assessment.

Sincerely,

Blaza Dean Moss

Blaza Dean Moss

Enclosure: resumé

Writing Resumes for the Intern Hopeful

C
APPENDIX

Resumés come in many different styles. However, I recommend a chronological style resumé because it lists all of your work experiences in dated order, and is very easy to read and follow. If you do not have a resumé, make certain that you draft one that's well crafted and thorough. Once you do this, all you have to do is update your information as time progresses and your information changes.

Some basic tips:

➤ **Make your "Objective" specific.** Direct your "Objective" in the resumé to each business or organization, so every resumé is "customized." This approach is better than using a generic "Objective" because it has a better appeal to the organization.

➤ **Use action words and adjectives.** When using these words appropriately, they can vividly describe your previous work experience that features related, positive contributions you made to other businesses or organizations.

➤ **Quantify your tasks.** List an approximate number to quantify the amount of work you produced, when you can. For instance, if you helped a company raise money, note how much. Example: I helped my company raise $10,000 during the annual fundraiser event.

➤ **Give yourself a title.** Give your internship positions an official title under the headings on your resumé. On my resumé for example, for my FBI Internship—I give myself the title of *Federal Law Enforcement Intern.* For my internship in Congress—*U.S. Congressional Intern.*

➤ **Use standard and professional email addresses—not a cute name or slang term.** During several of my internship experiences, I had the opportunity to review resumés of students that were seeking internships. I was surprised by how many applicants submitted resumés with unprofessional email addresses. A few fictional examples: Sexymary@circle.com, 2_Hott_4_You_Mary @circle.com, or BigBadJohnBoy@circle.com. Trust me when I say I've seen worse. Your resumé will be immediately trashed if you use similar unacceptable email addresses, and I have witnessed this many times before.

➤ **Use professional voicemail greetings.** The contact phone number you list should have a professional voicemail recording. Don't play music in the background, or record a joke, or any other inappropriate outgoing messages that would jeopardize your chance of obtaining the *professional* internship for which you applied.

➤ **Print on quality paper.** Your resumé should not be printed on "multi-purpose" copying or printing paper. Visit an office supply store, such as Office Max, and purchase quality resumé paper. Or, use high quality paper with a weight of 24 lb. and at least 25% cotton fiber. No loud or bright colors—I recommend the colors of white or ivory.

➢ **Don't include pictures.** Do not attach or insert your picture on your resumé, unless the application packet specifically states it as a requirement for submission.

➢ **Be concise.** Your resumé should be a succinct one-page document, unless you have enough solid experience for a two pager.[22] If you do require a longer resumé, it should list quality work experiences that will urge the reviewer to read on to the next page. Internship supervisors are contacted by many applicants and must review numerous resumés. As a result, they don't have a lot of time to read pages and pages about you. However, if your resumé is concise and very well crafted, your experiences will jump out at them, even from a quick glance by picking up on your buzzwords.

➢ **Use a consistent format.** The layout, spacing, and font should be consistent. Submitting a resumé that's in an inconsistent format conveys the notion that you are an unorganized and careless person

➢ **Don't make *any* mistakes or other typos.** There should be absolutely no spelling errors in your resumé. A resumé serves as a first impression, so you want to make it a good one!

See sample resumé on the following page.

---

[22] The sample resumé on the following page is one page, but it appears to be two due to the page format of this book.

Sample Resumé

Simoné Sane

Campus address:
163 University Lane
Cleveland, Ohio 44108
216-555-0000
sane@ssou.edu

Permanent address:
9849 West Park Drive
Cleveland, Ohio 44115
216-555-1111
sane1@circle.com

OBJECTIVE

Seeking an internship with Bloomberg Financial Executives Corporation to help execute its goals and mission by utilizing my education, professional skills, and other relevant experiences.

EDUCATION

Bachelor of Business Administration in Management
Expected May 2011
The Ohio State University
Columbus, Ohio
GPA 3.4/4.0

High School Diploma, College Prep Program
June 2007
Shaker Orange Academy
Shaker Heights, Ohio

RELEVANT COURSES
Strategic Management I & II
Accounting
Marketing

EXPERIENCE

Trust Corporation
Fall 2008
Business Development Intern

- Strategically developed a marketing proposal that increased revenues by $1,000,000
- Contacted over 500 customers in a telephone survey to solicit performance feedback
- Participated in five career fairs to recruit prospective employees

- Successfully managed, stocked, inventoried, and ordered large quantities of office supplies
- Assisted the staff with daily office operations (escorting visitors, answering phones, etc.)

SKILLS

- Proficient with business software and applications
- Proficient with all Microsoft Office applications
- Excellent communication, interpersonal, and leadership skills

AWARDS AND MEMBERSHIPS

- Recipient of "Most Dedicated Intern" award at Trust Corporation
- Member of C.H.A.N.G.E. Volunteers, Inc.
- Member of the Society of Young Business Administrators

REFERENCES

Available upon request.

Writing Personal Statements/Essays

D

APPENDIX

This Appendix covers my basic, but important principles to writing an effective personal statement essay. A personal statement is simply a very brief essay that tells agencies what your interests are and why they should hire you as an intern. Even though you may take it lightly, this is serious business. You can be on the dean's list and have excellent academic and work skills, but if you cannot write a solid essay, this deficiency will diminish your chances of obtaining an internship position.

The key to effective essay writing is investing the time to write one solid essay. Once this is accomplished you can build off of this essay over the years, similar to the expansion of a resumé.

Though this feat can be difficult, it is fun. I know this appears to be an oxymoron and you are probably wondering how something can be both hard and enjoyable. I think the task of writing a personal statement is both an art and science. It is an art because you must use your creativity to highlight your positive attributes, so they will stand out and separate you from the other applicants.

You will benefit by using analogies, metaphors, and quotes to validate your position in order to effectively persuade your reader. This involves using much creativity on your behalf. However, rather than following the instructions of a teacher to write creatively for fifteen minutes about how beautiful nature is, you get to write about yourself! This makes writing the essay much easier because no one knows you better than you know yourself. I believe that no one should be able to sell *you* better than you can sell yourself.

Writing this type of essay is also a science, as you need to determine a way to include a lot of information about yourself in one or two pages[23]. This was extremely tough for me at the beginning of my internship career because I did not know how to effectively include all of the necessary ingredients for a successful essay. Well, thank God for practice because I now know what it takes, and with *Learn to Intern CEO Style*, you can save a lot of time if you follow my guidelines.

I asked my supervisor at the internship with NASA's Office of the Inspector General—Office of Investigations how and why they selected me for the position over 15 other candidates. He told me that my essay was the best of them all. My personal statement writing skills were the number one reason I was awarded this particular internship[24].

Get this, he shared with me that a couple of the candidates had a 4.0 college grade point average and *still* didn't get the job over me. This is why I say you can be the smartest person in the world, but if you can't write a stellar personal statement, then your smarts really don't matter as much as you might think they do.

It's time for you to learn how to master one of the most popular essay questions[25], "Why do you want to intern with us?" This is a skill that you must learn because you usually need to sell yourself with one or two short pages of information. I know this is difficult and it's likely each one of us could probably write a book about ourselves; but they only want one or two pages of information. So what do you do?

---

[23] Sometimes the application requires it to be double-spaced and others single-spaced.

[24] I inserted this essay at the end of this appendix for your review.

[25] Oftentimes, there are other common, personal statement questions that interns are asked to answer. My basic tips should be able to help in answering those, as well.

Some basic tips:

> ➤ **Don't send a generic personal statement that you send to every other organization—make it agency-specific.** Make certain you incorporate the agency's name at least twice in the essay. Once in the introduction and again in the concluding paragraph. In addition, research the organization so you can include explicit examples of how your talents and ambitions are aligned with their mission and goals.

> ➤ **Answer all parts of the question specifically.** Don't go off on your own tangent and create your own topic by writing information about yourself that does not pertain to why you want the internship. This is one of the first opportunities employers have to measure how well you follow instructions. They often feel that if you cannot follow directions for a simple essay, then you sure would not be able to handle large projects.

> ➤ **Elaborate on why they should select *you* for the position.** As you know, a lot of other students are competing with you for internships. You want to explain to them how your skills will fit into their organizational values and mission. If you want to be a police officer, it isn't enough to say you want them to hire you as their intern because you've always dreamt of working for their agency. Or, because you watch every episode of *America's Most Wanted* and *Cops*. Instead, you might tell them how you possess a genuine desire to provide social justice and protection to the general public because this is an important American value that should be maintained.

> Also, if you had previous work or volunteer experiences, mention them. If not, be confident and express that you are a very quick learner and open to new experiences. Tell them you are confident in your talents and abilities to be an effective intern. You might also discuss any background experiences you feel may give you an edge over the next candidate. For example, make note of

some relevant classes that you have taken and how you can use what you've learned within their organization.

> ➢ **Be very careful not to exceed the page limits that are specified in the guidelines.** Unless the employer provides explicit standards on font size and style or margin and space settings, I recommend you using Times New Roman font—12 point, and margins set at 1.25 inches on all four sides, single-spaced. However, if more room is needed, you can minimize the font size to 11 or 11.5 and reduce the margins to 1 inch. This will buy you a little more space to add a few additional sentences.

> A word of caution: don't make your font so small that it's difficult to read. If that's the case, perhaps it's time to take another hard look and perform one more round of editing to delete some things so you can increase the font size. It's noteworthy to mention that you should always make certain your format is consistent when making adjustments and modifications.

See sample personal statement on the following page.

Submitting Academic Essays

If the employer requests a writing sample from one of your academic classes, make certain it is error free. Dig out one of your old graded essays and make all of the corrections that the instructor suggested. Actually, I would do this and have someone else (a friend, instructor, or the college's Writing Center) read it over again to make certain it is a solid essay.

Submit an essay that is neutral in any reference to religion or politics. These two topics are very touchy and some of your text just may offend your readers; on the other hand, it may not, but it's recommended to play this on the safe side. It may even be helpful to ask the employer which types of essays are acceptable and unacceptable for submission.

Sample Personal Statement

Why Want to Intern with the OIG[26]

I have an eager desire to procure a summer internship with NASA's Office of Inspector General (OIG) because I'm interested in pursuing a career in Federal law enforcement. Although any assignment in Federal law enforcement will satisfy me, working as part of a white-collar crime or government fraud team would be ideal. These types of crimes are often overlooked and considered frivolous by the public and many agencies. However, I have a dissenting opinion and think that these illicit activities should receive just as much time, energy, and resources as violent crimes.

From the time I was an elementary school student, I have been zealous for a career in law enforcement. Consequently, in high school I participated in a Criminal Justice Career and Technical Education program. Moreover, I continued to pursue my law enforcement career by majoring in Criminal Justice as an undergraduate student. Currently, I am pursuing a master's degree in public administration so I can become part of management in Federal law enforcement.

Since one's work experience is significant when applying for a job, it is incumbent upon me to receive substantive professional experience as a student. Hence, I have worked vigorously to ensure I had an opportunity to participate in paramount programs. In addition to working as a Federal security officer, some of my intern experiences have been with the Cleveland Metroparks Ranger Department (for two summers), Congressional Office of Congresswoman Stephanie Tubbs Jones, and Federal Bureau of Investigation.

Through these agencies and organizations, I have received training and professional experience that many of my peers have not. Though most of these internships were unpaid, I still opted to acquire an assignment. I hope that the Federal law enforcement agency I apply to for a career will recognize this and understand that I have a genuine desire to attain valuable work experience, so I can be more effective as an agent.

As an intern with the OIG, I hope to work with agents in an effort to thwart crime for our community. Furthermore, not only do I want to enhance my law enforcement attributes, but I also want to network with special agents and other professionals. During my prior internship experiences I didn't necessarily consider being part of management. However, through this internship, one of my primary goals will be to become more familiar with managers and learn effective skills from them that will provide a broader understanding in this area.

In conclusion, I am a disciplined and committed young man who, voted "Most Likely to Succeed" by my classmates, has been able to become educated, while maintaining my ability to positively influence my peers and gain the appreciated respect of many people. Mostly, I can offer the OIG the opportunity to invest in a talented individual who will give back what he learns to our community and government. I am receptive, an apt learner, inquisitive, responsible, affable, and

---

[26] I was instructed to write a one-page, single-spaced essay about why I wanted to intern with NASA's Office of the Inspector General.

committed to leading a positive life in the future. With my natural talents and acquired skills, I hope to make a difference to young people who are lacking role models. Not only will this internship afford me the great opportunity to continue pursuing my career in Federal law enforcement, but it will also further assist me in becoming a positive example to others within my community.

How to Master the Interview Process

E

Before the Interview

OK, you have secured an interview and now it is time for you to strategically communicate to the organization why you are their best candidate for the job. So now what?! Should you hurry and schedule a mock interview with your friend, instructor, or Career Services Department? If you say yes, you are right *and* wrong! In many instances, internship organizations will give you a short notice to come in for an interview. Considering this, it may be too late to set up a mock interview with someone.

To this end, I highly recommend you become very acquainted with your Career Services Department or career counselor well in advance of you even applying for internship positions. Request a preliminary appointment with one of these representatives. Share with them your interests to succeed and ask them what services they have that might be of benefit to you. If you are in college, the services should be plenty and most administrators will be delighted to assist you and pleased by your pro-activeness.

However, if you are in high school, there may only be one representative for the entire school and minimal services offered. But if you show a genuine interest in being successful, they should help you or at least point you in the right direction.

Also, it's important to know and have a general understanding about the vision, mission, and goals of the organization that will be interviewing you. Visit their website or go to the library to research the history and its current business. If you are unable to gather this information online or at the library, your last resort option is to call the organization to request materials to be mailed to you or made available for you to pick them up.

A few days or even the day before your actual interview, make sure you visit the interview site to ensure you know where it is. If you plan to catch the bus on the day of the interview, then take the bus there for a practice visit. If you are driving, make a prior trip, so you will become familiar with the route. I do not recommend actually going into the interview building, however. Doing this may give the organization the impression that you are over zealous.

When planning for your commute, take into consideration that there just may be a traffic jam or some other unexpected event that will delay your arrival time—so give yourself more time than usual to get there. On the day of the interview, you should arrive approximately 15 minutes early and stop in the bathroom one last time to check on your appearance (e.g. make certain no food is caught between your teeth). Finally, walk into the office with confidence and greet everyone you're introduced to with a smile and firm handshake.

During the Interview

You have heard the cliché, "You do not get a second chance to make a good first impression." And regardless as to whether it's fair or not, people will judge you based on how you look. This is why you must consciously do all you can in order to make your first impression a lasting one that glows. So how do you do it?

Some basic tips:

> **Dress professionally and appropriately.** Make certain
> your clothes are neutral in color, nicely pressed, and clean.
> Ladies shouldn't wear short-cut skirts or blouses. And for

the gentlemen, now isn't the time to wear tight shirts to flex your muscles. It's recommended that you visit a department clothing store to be measured for your exact suit and shirt size. Take the time to clean and shine your shoes. You don't want to dress as if you are going to a club or house party. Instead, dress for success—like you are business professional.

➢ **Be careful with your perfume and cologne fragrances.** I recommend that you do not wear any fragrance. If you do, it should be extremely mild. I am conservative and like to play things on the safe side—I suggest you play it safe too, as you do not want to be the source of the interviewer's sneezing fit because he/she is allergic to your smell. By the same token, you do not want to smell offensive or as if you haven't showered in a few days. Just simple hygiene should do the job. Make certain you use lotion on your hands and any other exposed skin.

➢ **Properly style and groom your hair.** Avoid wild or exotic hairstyles or colors. But if for some reason you feel that you can still get the job with an exotic hairstyle, make sure it's neat.

➢ **Don't wear flashy or large jewelry.** This goes for chains/necklaces, watches, medallions/charms, earrings, or bracelets. If you do wear jewelry, keep it simple.

➢ **Speak proper English, and no gum chewing.** Be articulate when you converse with others. Do not use slang terminology. Chewing gum or any other type of candy is extremely inappropriate, as well.

➢ **Make eye contact while you are speaking, and don't play with things.** Making eye contact demonstrates that you are confident and genuine with your remarks. While speaking (or not speaking) do not bite your nails, yawn, or play with anything (e.g. hair, pen or pencil, coins in your pocket, fingers, etc.) that could serve as a distraction during the interview.

> **Relax and be yourself in the interview and don't be ashamed of who you are.** Even if you are a little nervous, try your best not to demonstrate it. Also, don't be afraid to give honest answers about your values.

One question I distinctly remember in the Metroparks Ranger's internship interview was, "What is one of your biggest goals?" My answer was to grow in my spirituality. I was very aware that some people may have found that to be an inappropriate response, however, it was the truth. Now my answer would have been much different if the question was, "What is your biggest career or professional goal?"

But since the interviewer asked me a very general question, I decided to answer with that response—I was also aware that an employer couldn't discriminate against me due to my spirituality—so I felt comfortable with my answer. Later, one of the individuals on the interview panel mentioned that they were impressed by my answer and said there was nothing wrong my response.

No matter what question you get during your interview, just make sure you use a good judgment call, and never say anything that you think could potentially be blatantly offensive or inappropriate.

> **Show your interest in the position, and refer to interviewers by their names.** Figure out how to express that you are genuinely interested in the internship position, outside of the benefits it offers. You also want to refer to interviewers by their names because people enjoy hearing the sound of their name—trust me, you will get a few extra points for doing this!

> **Small talk should always be neutral and professional.** Unless it is definitely related to the internship you are applying for, never talk about politics, religion, or any other category that you think could create some type of bias or

tension between you and the organization. Topics such as the weather or sports are typically much safer to discuss.

➢ **Maintain a good sitting posture.** Don't slouch or sit as if you are sitting outside at a family picnic. Sit properly because this expresses that you are attentive and interested in the position.

➢ **Don't operate cell phones and/or iPods.** Your cell phone should be turned off; no, not even on vibrate. *Never* look at your phone or wristwatch during the interview. As a matter of fact, if you drove, you might consider leaving your cell phone in the car. Looking at your phone and watch conveys that you are ready to go, bored, or impatient—a very rude impression. Also, there's no need for you to bring out your iPod or MP3 Player for any reason, either.

➢ **Decline to accept any beverages or snacks.** The only thing I encourage you to take is water, if it is offered. I don't recommend asking unless you *really* need a drink. Water is clean in the event of an accidental spill. Other spilled beverages could destroy a person's clothes, paperwork, or prove to be tough to quickly clean up.

I would not accept any food because it may be sticky or you may get something caught between your teeth (how embarrassing!), or the interviewer will invariably ask a question as soon as your mouth is full of food.

General questions you should expect to encounter

1. Can you tell me about yourself?

2. What do you know about our organization?

3. Which classes have you taken that relate to this position or organization?
4. What are some of your goals?

5. How computer proficient are you?

6. How are your multi-tasking skills?

7. Can you share with me a problem you have experienced and how you solved it?

8. What's your biggest weakness?

9. Why should I hire you for this position?

10. Are you often late or ever absent from work or class?

How you should respond to these questions

You never want to simply answer these questions with one-word answers. This is your chance to shine. This is where you sell yourself. Your resumé paved the way to your interview; now it's up to you to use your communication and salesmanship skills to obtain the internship.

But—know when to conclude. Going on too long about yourself in any one question (or all of them!) risks 1) The interviewer becoming bored and annoyed, and 2) Talking until you inadvertently say something you wish you hadn't. If you talk too long—and they let you—nervous energy often takes over, and it *will* happen!

Explain yourself and speak with confidence. Make eye contact with the interviewer and eliminate the "ums," "likes," and "you know what I means." If you need to think about an answer, ask if they mind allowing you to take a couple of seconds to consider your response. Taking a moment to gather your thoughts is better than trying to ramble off, resulting in an ineffective answer.

It's also important to note that you want to learn the name of the person (or people) who is conducting the interview, so you can refer to them by name when responding to, or asking, intelligent questions.

Lastly, be prepared for them to throw a crazy question at you like, "If you were an animal, which one would you be and why?" Some interviewers ask surprising questions like this, and others don't. Just be prepared because they want to gauge how well you deal with unexpected situations. A generic response could be—"I would be a dog—because just as they say, "a dog is a man's best friend," I am loyal to my work and whatever else I commit myself to. Consequently, I will be like a best friend to the internship program."

Questions you should ask during your interview

It's vitally important that you ask questions whenever you have the opportunity to do so during the interview. Asking intelligent questions demonstrates that you are seriously interested in the internship and not afraid to communicate with others, in a professional setting.

It's important to preface the questions that you will see below with the statement, "If I were to be selected for the position ..." For example, "If I were to be selected for the position, what would be your expectations of me?" Doing this shows that you are humble and aren't automatically assuming that a position will be offered to you.

You will not have the chance to ask all of these questions since you may have already received some of this information. But, if some of these questions have not been answered when they ask you if you have any questions, then ask them.

1. What would be your expectations of me?

2. What would be my responsibilities?

3. What would be my work schedule? Is it flexible?

4. Are there any examples of how previous interns succeeded in this position?

5. Are there any examples of how previous interns failed in this position?

6. Are there any training or professional development opportunities available that would help me to do the job more effectively?

7. What benefits would this internship provide to my career future?

8. What has your experience been like with this organization?

9. What are some pros and cons about this internship position?

10. Are there any past interns I may speak with to discuss their past internship experiences with this organization?

If you are unaware of the monetary benefits that come with the internship, save this question for last. This way the interviewer will not think that money and benefits are all that interest you. As a last question, you may ask, "Are there any compensatory benefits that the internship offers to students?"

During the interview you must exude confidence and smile, which can be accomplished by practicing and believing in yourself. Practice answering the questions, but don't attempt to memorize your responses. You want your responses to sound natural, not scripted, during the interview.

Tips on What to do After Your Interview

F

Within 24-hours, send a thank-you letter to your interviewer (s), rather than a card or email because this gesture is more formal and appropriate. The most important part about this is writing something specific about what was discussed during the interview—this information should be placed in the first paragraph.

The next paragraph should state why you want the position and how your skills match their interests. Indicate again, your desire to attain the position in the following paragraph. You should close your letter by stating that you will follow-up with a phone call to offer additional information. Make sure you sign your name in black or blue ink right above your typed name in your conclusion.

Your thank-you letter should not be printed on "multi-purpose" copying or printing paper. Visit an office supply store, such as Office Max, for high quality paper with a weight of 24 lb. and at least 25% cotton fiber. No loud or bright colors—I recommend the colors of white or ivory. The envelope for your thank-you letter should be of the same quality and color paper as your letter. Do not attach or insert your picture on your thank-you letter.

See sample thank-you letter that I've used in the past on the next page.

Follow-up after your interview

At the conclusion of your interview, ask the interviewer when you should expect to hear from them. They may say that within a week they will call, send a letter, or email you with a response to the interview. Do not contact them unless at least a week (five business days) has passed and you have not yet heard anything. If they give a specific date when they will make a decision, wait until a day after that date to contact them. I recommend calling the person who interviewed you to check the status of their decision. You might say something like, "Hello, my name is A'Malley Michael and I interviewed with you last Monday. I'm calling to check on the status of your decision for the internship position."

If they indicate to you that they offered the position to someone else, still be professional and thank them for their time. Let them know that you are still interested in future opportunities, if something should become available.

Sample Thank-You Letter

5 Old Ridge Circle Road Apt. #134
East Cleveland, Ohio 44112
216-555-5835
a.m.moss08@circle.edu

August 30, 2007

Mr. Kreitler Summerday
Director of Health Programs
Urban Health Center
36 Euclid Avenue
Cleveland, Ohio 44115

Dear Mr. Summerday:

I appreciate the time you took from your busy schedule to meet with me last Friday. I deeply value the information you shared with me concerning urban healthcare issues and why they should be ameliorated.

As a product of an underserved metropolitan area, I inherently share some of the same concerns you addressed, about healthcare disparities. In addition, my effective communication skills and public policy development experiences have well-prepared me for this internship position. I know this project is going to be great for our city, and I would value the opportunity to be a part of it.

If you believe I am qualified for this graduate assistantship position, I would greatly appreciate hearing from you.

Thank you again for the interview and your consideration. I hope to meet with you again soon. I will give you a phone call in the near future to see if you need any additional information about me, to complete your assessment.

Sincerely,

Antoine D. Moss

Antoine D. Moss

Tips on What to do When You Decline a Position

G
APPENDIX

If you are offered a position and aren't certain if you would like the job, ask if you may have a few days to consider the offer. I know you are thinking why in the world you would want to turn down an internship offer. Well, as you become more experienced and apply for several internships at once, you just may receive a couple of simultaneous offers. If this happens you would have to consider from which one you would likely gain the most valuable experience. If the organization offers you some time to think about it, you can receive help in determining this decision by talking to your Career Services representatives or mentors about your options.

Once you have determined which internship you want to pursue, contact this organization and let them know your decision. You should also contact the interviewer of the one you've decided against, by phone. Advise them that you will not take the position. Do not simply leave a message with a secretary or by voicemail, stating your decision.

You want to personally speak with them to discuss this matter, then follow up your call with a letter (mailed via the U.S. Postal Service) that officially declines the position. In both the conversation and letter, thank them for their time and offer of the position. Let them also know that you would be receptive to a future internship or even full-time position.

Letter format—in the first paragraph you should thank the organization and let them know why you are declining the internship. In the last paragraph you can thank them again, saying something specific about the organization, and close by indicating the possibility of you applying for a future position. Make sure you sign your name in black or blue ink right above your typed name, to close the letter.

Your job decline letter should not be printed on "multi-purpose" copying or printing paper. Visit an office supply store, such as Office Max, and purchase high quality paper with a weight of 24 lb. and at least 25% cotton fiber. Do not attach or insert your picture on your letter.

See sample job decline letter that I've used in the past on the following page.

Making the phone call and writing a letter are important actions you want to make, as it creates a positive reflection on your good, professional image. For all you know, you may apply there again next year for an internship or job, after graduation. You just never know what the future holds, so professionalism is an essential leadership trait for your successful future.

Sample Job Offer Decline Letter

5 Old Ridge Circle Road Apt. #134
East Cleveland, Ohio 44112
216-555-5835
a.m.moss08@circle.edu

April 14, 2006

Ms. Kyralynne Brownard
Program Officer
The Cleveland Leaders Institute
22 Pine Oak Street Suite 130
Cleveland, Ohio 44115

Dear Ms. Brownard:

Thank you very much for the opportunity to interview for the Cleveland Leaders Institute Internship Program. However, I must respectfully decline your kind offer. While I was highly interested in participating in your summer internship program, I recently accepted a position with another organization. At this time, this position appeared to align more closely with my career goals and aspirations.

Again, I would like to thank the Cleveland Leaders Institute for taking the time to consider me for an internship position. I am very impressed with the mission of this organization and wish that I could have been a part of your continuing success. Should I seek employment or an internship in the future, I would not hesitate to apply again to the Cleveland Leaders Institute.

Sincerely,

Antoine D. Moss

Antoine D. Moss

Starting an Internship Conceptual Framework

H

Below you will read a written explanation for the Starting an Internship Conceptual Framework. You can view a visual depiction of this internship search process on the next page.

You are the powerful link between your internship organization and school. You should be in good standing with both of these institutions because you want to build healthy relationships with them. This is so because the internship and your school represent locks that need to be unlocked in order to achieve success with your goals.

Once you "MapQuest" your internship, you will have the key to open the locks that will ultimately provide access to your goals. MapQuesting your internship simply means that you must map out how you would like to get to your specified destination during your internship. Your destination is your goals, so you must figure out what steps you need to take to achieve them by developing an Internship Plan. A sample Internship Plan can be found in Appendix J.

It's important for you to know that your goals should be in alignment with the goals of your internship and school.

Starting an Internship
Conceptual Framework

Intern CEO Style
Internship Plan

I
APPENDIX

In order to *Intern CEO Style*, it is essential for you to develop an Internship Plan. Writing an internship plan is similar to mapping a geographical location to which a person desires to commute, that's why I refer to this process as a MapQuest. The directional search simply tells one how to get from destination A to destination B. You want to set goals for yourself along with action steps that highlight how you plan to execute them in order for you to get from point A to point B. Also, it's important for you to set a timeline for attaining your goals. Goal timelines can help you stay on track and hold you accountable for your goals, during a specified timeframe.

To begin, you should discover your brand or competitive edge, just as any business entity would. A brand is oftentimes centered on a skill that comes easily or naturally to a person. Or, it can be an attribute that you don't posses inherently, but consciously endeavor to improve over time.

Identifying one or a few dominate skills that can be rolled up into your brand doesn't mean you do not have other strengths. To

181

this end, you must continuously sharpen your other strengths *and* weaknesses too.

Asking yourself *what* benefits or value you want to extract from your internship in a *broad* sense, should help you develop a vision. And your personal mission statement should emphasize *how* you will attain your vision, while you are performing at your internship.

For example, your vision may perhaps be written as follows, "To enhance my professional skills so I can become a better student-leader." As a mission you could state, "To expand my network and produce quality work by interacting well with others and completing assigned tasks to the best of my abilities."

See one of my previous *Intern CEO Style* Internship Plans on the following page.

Antoine D. Moss
Intern CEO Style Internship Plan
NASA Glenn Research Center

Brand
Demonstrate proficient communication and interpersonal skills. Over the years, I have learned that I am fortunate to have excellent communication and interpersonal skills. As a brand, I want to be recognized as having these exceptional soft-social skills that I utilize, to work effectively with others.

Vision
To excel as a professional, collegiate, and community leader through internships, while empowering others.

Mission
To optimize my talents by offering positive commitment, integrity, energy, and innovation in hopes of contributing significantly to the NASA Glenn Research Center's mission.

---

1. Goal: Offer innovative ideas to scheduled work assignments and processes.

Action Steps: Think outside the box and develop new ways to improve the operations that fall under the area of my responsibilities.

Timeline: Within due date of assignments and/or projects.

----

2. Goal: Gain a practical understanding of public sector management.

Action Steps: Shadow and interview members of middle and senior management.

Timeline: By October 12, 2008.

----

3. Goal: Become engaged in public outreach and community affairs.

Action Steps: Represent NASA at three career fairs and other community school events.

Timeline: By December 17, 2008.

----

4. Goal: Network and become visible throughout the NASA Glenn Research Center.

Action Steps: Attend three organizational and Center social functions. Join planning committees for activities.

Timeline: By February 15, 2009.

----

5. Goal: Empower other students and interns.

Action Steps: Assist and make myself available to help and mentor other student interns.

Timeline: As the opportunities present themselves.

Other comments by intern: I will do my absolute best to adhere to this Internship Plan, in order for me to optimize my experience with NASA. I will demonstrate the highest level of professionalism at all times, in order to effectively represent myself and NASA.

Other comments by supervisor: I will offer my time, expertise, and any other needed resources to make certain Antoine has the opportunity to succeed in this internship.

_____   _____

Intern's Signature   Supervisor's Signature

_____   _____

Date   Date

Tips on What to do After Your Internship is Over

J

APPENDIX

Whether you enjoyed your internship or not, you should mail the organization a thank-you letter within a week after the internship concludes. In the first paragraph, thank the organization, and write about a business related activity that you enjoyed. In the next paragraph, offer your assistance to help future interns that will be employed by the respective organization. The following paragraph should state that you have included your updated resumé with the letter.

Also, express your desire to attain a future full-time position or internship, if this is the case. For the concluding paragraph, let them know you will be in touch, and thank them again. Make sure you sign your name in black or blue ink right above your typed name, to close the letter.

Your internship thank-you letter should not be printed on "multi-purpose" copying or printing paper. Visit an office supply store, such as Office Max, and purchase high quality paper with a weight of 24 lb. and at least 25% cotton fiber. No loud or bright colors—I recommend the colors of white or ivory. Do not attach or insert your picture on your letter.

See sample thank-you letter on the following page.

Sample Thank-You Letter

123 Treemount Lane
Pittsburgh, PA 15205
412-555-7600
brad382@circle.com

June 27, 2009

Ms. Mayanne Redder
Internship Program Manager
National Savers Bank
678 Blueberry Lane
Pittsburgh, PA 15205

Dear Ms. Redder:

I would like to thank you and the rest of the organization for developing a very successful and empowering internship for me at National Savers Bank. I truly enjoyed formulating marketing ideas and actually being able to implement them. The community outreach events were also beneficial because I was able to utilize my communication skills to attract new customers and employees.

I am well aware of the time that it took everyone at National Savers Bank to invest in me as an intern. This internship has definitely helped me become a better team player by involving me in so many collaborative efforts. Consequently, please feel free to have future interns contact me should they need any guidance, advice, or help during their internship experience.

Just for your records and reference, I have enclosed my updated resumé. I would appreciate any direction on acquiring future internship opportunities or full-time positions with National Savers Bank, or other similar enterprises.

As I have cultivated some personal and professional relationships with employees at National Savers Bank, I will be in touch periodically. Thank you again for such a rewarding experience, and please feel free to share this letter with the employees throughout the company.

Sincerely,

Bradley Adamsmith

Bradley Adamsmith

Enclosure: resumé.

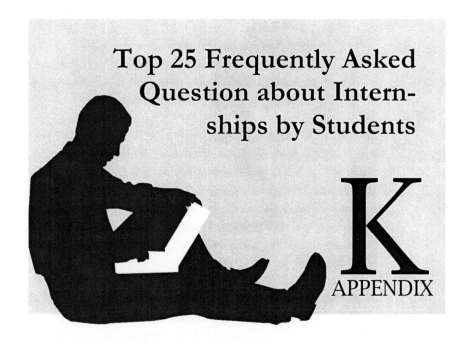

Top 25 Frequently Asked Question about Intern-ships by Students

K
APPENDIX

1. **What is an internship?**
   An internship is a structured experience that's usually formulated with an agreement by the student, their school, and a professional organization. Internships give students the opportunity to gain substantive work experience, while they apply theories and lessons learned in the classroom to a real workplace setting.

2. **Do I have to be super-smart to get an internship?**
   No! You must, however, be a serious student who's dedicated to your career success. You need to have the desire to learn and sharpen your skills so you can effectively contribute to internship organizations.

3. **How can I find an internship?**
   You can learn about or find internships by consulting with your resources, such as librarians, school administra-

tors, mentors, family members, friends, and through Internet research.

4. ***When should I begin looking for internships?***
Most applications for internships have to be submitted four to five months before the actual start of the internship, so you have to carefully plan your activities.

Example timeline: A) Begin internship search on September 1, 2010. B) Identify an internship(s) to apply to. Start completing the application process and gathering all of the required documents and materials (e.g. transcripts and recommendation letters) on November 1, 2010. C) Submit your internship application by the deadline date of February 1, 2011. E) Begin internship on the start date of June 1, 2011.

However, I must note that some internship application processes are so extensive to where you may have to begin applying and collecting the necessary information and documents up to a year in advance.

5. ***Do I have to find an internship through my school?***
It depends on your school's process. I would recommend checking with your Career Services counselors or representatives to ensure you are adhering to their guidelines. This is important because you don't want to complete an internship and your school later notifies you that it will not count for academic credit, since you didn't follow their internship protocol.

6. ***Are all internships the same?***
Just like there are many different colleges and universities, there are many different types of internships. Interns can shadow professionals or be more directly involved by performing basic duties. Some internships require students to write a final essay or regularly report to an instructor, to receive academic credit. Some are paid and others are unpaid. However, internships are typically the

same in that they afford students the opportunity to gain practical work experience.

7. How can I recognize good versus bad internship opportunities?

Good internship opportunities are typically well structured and allow interns to engage in productive and substantive work assignments. Bad internships generally provide interns with little to no guidance and supervision. They are often a thin disguise for temporary secretarial help, and don't provide students opportunities to enhance and develop their professional skills. But, you must still find something good or valuable in *bad* internships, as well.

8. Should I participate in an internship with an organization that doesn't have a big name?

Yes! Whether you participate in an internship that is sponsored by a well-known organization or one that is of a lower profile, internships are valuable experiences.

9. Why should I accept an unpaid internship?

Just like paid internships, unpaid internships can be invaluable experiences. If employers witness you working hard for free, they are often more assured that you would perform even better for compensation. Generally speaking, completing any type of internship will give you a competitive advantage over your peers.

10. What if I can't afford an unpaid internship?

If you can't afford to participate in an unpaid internship, I recommend trying to do whatever you can to make it work. Internships typically last only a few months, but their benefits can last forever so make the sacrifice, if you can.

11. Should I still apply to an internship if I don't meet the minimum qualifications?

Yes! If you think you have what it takes to be an excellent intern, but you don't quite meet the required grade point average or other specified qualifications, still apply. Usually, there are numerous variables considered before one is eliminated from the application pool. You definitely will not acquire the internship if you don't apply. On the other hand, if you do apply, you just *may* get it.

12. *Have you ever had multiple internship offers?*
Yes, I've been offered multiple internships, simultaneously. I was able to place myself in this position by attaining many other top internships and performing well in them. When I received multiple offers I thoroughly analyzed the positions and consulted with my mentors for their advice, before making a final decision.

13. *Were you ever rejected from an internship?*
Yes, I've been rejected from an internship on more than one occasion. However, I learned from my mistakes and maintained a positive attitude while pursuing other internship opportunities.

14. *How do I overcome anxiety or fears I may have before beginning or even pursuing internship opportunities?*
You can overcome any anxiety or fears by keeping in mind the end result—valuable experience—and not being afraid to succeed. Internships are stepping-stones to your future, and great opportunities for students to grow. You shouldn't be afraid of that at all. You will make mistakes, but everyone does. Just be receptive and learn from them. Your internship supervisor, Career Services representative, family, and friends should be able to encourage you to succeed and lessen your anxiety.

15. *Were you ever intimidated by an internship?*
Yes, in the beginning of my internship career I was anxious about my second internship with a law enforcement department. However, by the end of this internship, my confidence was boosted to the point that future internship anxieties and fears were lessened.

16. **Why can't my first internship be in the career of my dreams?**

It's possible that you will not attain your dream internship early on in your internship career. Your dream internship is probably extremely competitive, so you will need to work hard at other internships and learn the necessary skills that will help you obtain your *dream* internship.

17. **How can I Intern CEO Style?**

To *Intern CEO Style* you must understand that you are the Creator of Excellent Opportunities. You must be proactive and dedicated to being the best intern you can be, in order to fully prepare for your career. This comes with a lot of rewarding hard work and sacrifice, while maintaining a stellar reputation and work ethic. The *Intern CEO Style* framework has five primary pillars, you must: 1) Develop yourself as a business, 2) Take personal responsibility over your internship career by customizing your experiences, 3) Consistently produce quality work, 4) Sharpen your soft-social skills and become a "people person," and 5) Always maintain your integrity.

18. **How should I cope with a boring internship?**

Some internships are more exciting than others, however, internships are what you make them. You must maintain a positive disposition while performing any type of assignment. If you are performing boring work, you should work hard at these tasks and prepare yourself for bigger projects. Oftentimes, internship supervisors want to get a feel for your work style and performance with menial tasks before they will entrust you with work assignments that are extremely important to the organization.

19. **How should I handle problems at my internships?**

As an intern, you never want to be at the center of a problem. If you encounter any type of dilemma, you should consult with your internship supervisor and/or your school's internship point of contact. Don't gossip or talk to your coworkers about problems because this could cause many undesirable rumors to spread.

20. **How do I prepare myself to be successful during my internship?**

You can prepare yourself for success by speaking with your internship supervisor, mentors, and school Career Services representatives to seek their advice. They should be able to offer tips about how to achieve success. And of course, periodically referring to *Learn to Intern CEO Style* will be extremely helpful, as well!

21. **How can I improve my resumé or interviewing skills?**

You can improve your resumé, interviewing, or any other relevant career skills by consulting with your school's Career Services representative or librarian. You can also conduct some independent research on the Internet to enhance these essential skills.

22. **What is a mentor?**

A mentor is someone you trust and can depend on to provide valuable advice about your academic and professional career. A mentor can be a family friend, teacher, peer, or an individual from the professional environment. If you think someone would be a good mentor for you, simply ask them if they are willing to serve as your mentor.

23. **Do I have to be a U.S. Citizen to obtain an internship?**

Most internships in the U.S. require interns to be a U.S. citizen. However, one should inquire with respective internship organizations for their citizenship requirements.

24. **Do internship organizations look at my Facebook or other social networking pages to decide if they will hire me or not?**

Yes! There are some organizations that review social networking webpages and accounts of prospective interns before making a hiring decision. So you should be careful with the pictures and comments you post online—you don't want to risk missing out on a career opportunity due inappropriate postings.

25. ***How can I obtain a free graduate degree?***
Graduate assistantships typically offer students a tuition grant or waiver, along with a stipend. The stipend may not be a lot of money, but your education will be paid for. Oftentimes, students pick up a weekend job if they desire to earn extra income. In addition to graduate assistantships, if you have a full-time job that will not allow you to acquire an assistantship, some employers may offer tuition reimbursement options.